P9-CBF-917

# The

# ULTIMATE
# GARDENER

## The Best Experts' Advice for Cultivating a Magnificent Garden with Photos and Stories

Charlie Nardozzi

of the National Garden Association

Health Communications, Inc.
HCI Books, the Life Issues Publisher
Deerfield Beach, Florida

*www.hcibooks.com*
*www.ultimatehcibooks.com*

We would like to acknowledge the writers and photographers who granted us permission to use their material. Copyright credits for interior photographs appear on each photograph, and credits for literary work are listed alphabetically by authors' last names. Contact information as supplied by the photographers and writers can be found in the back matter of this book.

*Creating Theme Gardens with Children.* © Linda E. Allen. All rights reserved.

*Valentines in the Garden.* © Linda E. Allen. All rights reserved.

*The Garden Saved My Life.* © Barbara Blossom Ashmun. All rights reserved.

*(Copyright credits continued on page 247)*

Library in Congress Cataloging-in-Publication Data
is available through the Library of Congress.

Publisher: Health Communications, Inc.
      3201 S.W. 15th Street
      Deerfield Beach, FL 33442-8190

*Cover Design: Larissa Hise Henoch*
*Cover Photo: ©Purestock*
*Photo Editor: Justin Rotkowitz*
*Interior Design: Lawna Patterson Oldfield*

*To Leslie Goldman,*
*The Enchanted Gardener,*
*for planting dreams and*
*seeds of inspiration.*

*To all those who garden*
*and for those who dream to*
*have a garden one day.*

# Is something "Ultimately" important to you? Then we want to know about it. . . .

We hope you enjoyed *The Ultimate Gardener*. We are planning many more books in the Ultimate series, each filled with entertaining stories, must-know facts, and captivating photos. We're always looking for talented writers to share slice-of-life true stories, creative photographers to capture images that a story can't tell, as well as top experts to offer their unique insights on a given topic.

For more information on submission guidelines, or to suggest a topic for an upcoming book, please visit the Ultimate website at **www.ultimatehcibooks.com**, or write to: Submission Guidelines, Ultimate Series, HCI Books, 3201 SW 15th St., Deerfield Beach, FL 33442.

For more information about other books by Health Communications, Inc., please visit **www.hcibooks.com**.

# Contents

## Garden Transformations

## Through the Seasons

## Memory Gardens

# Feeding the Soul

# Garden Variety

# Must-Know Info

# Introduction

Gardening is an activity everyone, from all walks of life, can enjoy. From kids planting their first bean to senior citizens growing heirloom flowers in containers, gardening is a lifelong hobby that fulfills many needs. We all know gardens are beautiful to look at and the food they produce tasty to eat, but consider other ways they enhance our lives. Gardens are a great way to reduce our energy consumption, reduce pollution, and provide more green space in our communities.

Gardens provide habitat for animals, birds, bees, and a whole host of other creatures. Perhaps most important, gardens provide a respite from our busy days. You can't put a price tag on the peace and serenity puttering in a garden at the end of the day can bring.

Gardens also bring people together. It's common ground. As a writer for the National Gardening Association, I've traveled across the country visiting gardeners from all walks of life. Regardless of our political, religious, or personal differences, whenever we started to talk gardening, we came together in the simple love of growing plants.

Gardening is also a way to teach kids about the environment, our culture, and academic subjects such as math and science. Kids light up when they grow plants for themselves. In the process of hands-on learning in the garden, kids are taught the personal and academic skills that will help them throughout their lives. At National Gardening we have found that when kids participate in gardening programs, they score better on academic tests, develop better team and interpersonal skills, and have healthier attitudes about exercise and nutritious eating. Plus, there's nothing like the expression on a kid's face when they realize that carrots grow underground, when they pick their first bean from a plant they grew from seed, or when they chomp into a vine-ripened cherry tomato for the first time. All the classroom teaching in the world on nutrition and ecology can't substitute for the real-world experience of growing and eating your own food or seeing a butterfly sip nectar from a flower.

I know firsthand that gardening is a way to stay connected with family and friends. I grew up in the shadow of my Italian grandfather's farm. As a kid I remember helping pick apples and weed potatoes. My garden memories primarily revolve around food. Fresh, healthy, organic (even though we didn't call it that back then) food was raised for our Italian family meals. They filled our bellies and our souls. Meals were a way to be together as a family and a community. Today, we find more and more people turning to edible gardening to produce some of their own food. People are yearning for more connection with one another, and growing and sharing fresh produce is a way to get there. Growing our own food also saves money, makes us feel more secure knowing what was sprayed (or not sprayed) on the vegetables and fruits, and helps us contribute to a reduction in our carbon footprint by buying less food shipped hundreds of miles from the farm to our grocery stores.

Gardens can also help rebuild communities. Community gardens in urban areas often start as a small project by a few dedicated local people to grow a little food or a patch of flowers. However, what often happens is that a small project excites the neighborhood and it turns into a beautification and community revival program that cleans up empty lots, creates green park space, creates stronger community cohesion, reduces crime, and increases property values.

So gardens are more than just pretty flowers and tasty vegetables and fruits. More than 82 million households or 71 percent of the U.S. population gardened in 2007. These people know that spending a little time in the yard tending a vegetable or flower garden, planting a tree or shrub, or mowing a lawn not only makes for a more beautiful and healthier world, but creates a more relaxing, peaceful, and connected life in our families, neighborhoods, and country.

I hope you enjoy these stories about the trials and tribulations of gardening. At the end of this book, read through the Must-Know Info to get specific ideas for your garden. If you're still looking for more information on gardening, visit the National Gardening Association's website (www.garden.org) to learn about home gardening and gardening with kids. Above all, spend a little time in the garden every day to relax and ground yourself in this timeless, rejuvenating hobby.

# Acknowledgments

'd like to thank all of the gardeners who shared their personal stories with us. Some are heartwarming, some sad, some amusing, but all of them illustrate how gardening can touch our lives.

# Cultivating
# Humor

# A Heartwarming Day in the Garden

### By Linda Kaullen Perkins

My gardening fever had started way back in January with the arrival of the first seed catalog. Finally, on this spring-like Saturday, I could turn my attention to our gardening spot. Last year's treelike weeds saluted me with round, sticky burrs—the kind that could deliver paralyzing pain to human flesh. These monsters had to be destroyed by fire.

My husband, the other half of the Weed Warrior Team, had just received an emergency call from his employer, the railroad. It was up to me to tackle the garden spot alone. What could be so hard about that?

With rake and matches in hand, I walked to the scraggly brown plot next to the orchard. My horse, ears pointed, peeked around the corner of her shelter. "Hi, Ginger," I called. She lumbered around the shed closer to the fence for a better view.

My first attempt at starting a fire fizzled like a dud firecracker. I raked some debris into two small piles and tried again. Two little fires sputtered, burned a few minutes, and puffed up in a trail of smoke. At this rate, I would never get these weeds annihilated.

Instead of raking up piles, I lit lots of little fires and waited to see if they would spread. Before long, flames licked the air and started taking off in several directions. Within minutes, uneasiness crept over me. Why hadn't I taken precautions before starting my burning project? I ran toward the house, which by now seemed miles away. I struggled with three hoses coiled like snakes outside the basement door. At the spigot nearest the garden, I attached a hose and ran with the other free end. The hoses stretched many yards short of my goal. I needed to find two more hoses. Nothing like planning ahead. Since I was halfway between the garden and the house, I debated: should I go check the fire or go back to the basement and get more hoses?

Once more, I raced to the garden spot. To my horror, fire whipped over a large area. I started stomping around the edges. "Where did that wind come from?" I shouted. "It could burn the whole orchard. Or the horse's shed! Do horses really run toward fire?"

I had to get more hoses. My heart pounded as I ran to the basement, flinging open the door. I sped past the phone and grabbed the hoses. I stopped, backtracked to the phone, and reached for the card with the phone numbers for the Volunteer Fire Department.

"I have this minor grass fire," I said, trying to keep panic out of my voice. "I could use some help. Please ask someone to bring one little truck. Don't bring that big truck!"

One little fire truck, eight pickups, and twelve farmers later, the fire was out.

"Now remember, gentlemen, you don't need to mention this to anyone." Of course, they knew who I meant when I said "anyone."

Later that afternoon, my husband walked in the door with a

smirk on his face and said, "What have you been up to today?"

"You already know," I said. "Who told you?"

"You mean when I got flagged down on the blacktop?"

I made a face.

He hooked his thumbs in his overalls. "Let me put it this way," he said. "Someone offered three words of advice."

"And what were those words of wisdom?" I asked.

"Junior told me to hide the matches."

# The Hardy Mum Incident

*By Christine E. Collier*

One early autumn day as my husband and I drove past our garden center, he asked, "Why do they always advertise hardy mums for sale? Don't they ever sell regular mums?"

I had to laugh, as I had wondered the same thing many times. "I guess they want you to know they're hardy enough to withstand a frost," I replied.

I love autumn mums, whether growing in a garden, alongside a mailbox, or sitting on a porch. There are more and more beautiful shades of color available each year. Most gardens in the East look pretty bleak by the start of autumn, and mums extend the season.

I buy many colors and set them on our brick steps by the front door. I add a few pumpkins and my little scarecrow, and I have an autumn display that will last until Thanksgiving.

This particular autumn I bought a beautiful rose-colored mum plant for five dollars at our garden center. It was healthy and covered in blooms. I wanted to buy more, but feeling thrifty that day, I didn't. A few days later while shopping, I saw a large display in front of my grocery store with a sign that read "Hardy Mums—5 for $10."

They were in desperate need of water. Someone had neglected them terribly. I felt I could bring them back to life. They were covered in buds and the plants were green. They had just enough blooms that I could tell each color. I chose five: cream, deep burgundy, yellow, gold, and a gorgeous pale mauve. That was the beginning of what I like to call the Hardy Mum Incident. Can you tell I'm a mystery writer?

I watered my new plants frequently, took off the dead buds and leaves, and waited for the explosion of color. Each morning I opened our front door and cautiously peeked out at my mums. At first, I was very patient. I knew they were in distress because of lack of water. It would take time. My husband shook his head and chuckled as if to say "dream on." My children would comment as they left the house, "Why do you have dead plants sitting on the front steps?"

As the weeks went by, my mumbling grew. "I could've bought two healthy plants for ten dollars instead of five half-dead, worthless ones." I learned a valuable lesson. I tried to save a little and ended up with nothing! I complained that I should return them to the grocery store. The new buds never opened; they simply dried up and fell off.

"Grocery stores don't know how to take proper care of plants," I ranted.

This tirade went on for quite a while. I'd walk into the living room, look out our front door, and shake my head in disgust. Finally, one morning in late autumn there were a few bright yellow blooms on one of the plants. Perhaps three. "They're starting to bloom," I yelled. My husband smiled, but it was a pity smile.

Early the next morning I got ready to go to the grocery store. I didn't bother checking the plants. My husband decided to go with me. We have a drive-in garage and a long driveway. As he slowly backed down the drive, I looked toward our house. "Honey, look! The yellow plant is covered in blooms; it looks like it's doubled. Why, it's almost a miracle."

"Really," he said coyly. "Why do you say that?"

"Look, even from this distance I can see the blooms! There were just a few yesterday and you could barely see them. It's covered now."

He smiled. I'd seen that smile before.

It hit me instantly. "It's either a miracle or someone's playing tricks."

He burst out laughing. He works second shift, and on his supper hour the night before, he had bought a perfect yellow mum plant. Late that night after he got home, he replaced my sickly yellow mum with the new one.

"This is the first morning you haven't looked out the front door and complained," he said. "I've been waiting for that all morning."

"Yes," I answered, "but this worked out even better. I would've known immediately it was a new plant up close, the first clue being it's double in size. This way, looking from the middle of our long driveway, the size wasn't so noticeable. This was a pretty darn clever trick." My husband agreed and, still laughing, said, "Your reaction was absolutely priceless."

"I only wish one thing, but I'm not complaining," I said. "Yellow was my least favorite of all the colors there."

"You're kidding. I looked all over for yellow because that was the one you mentioned had new blooms, and I wanted you to think it was the same plant."

Moral of this story: bargains are sometimes not what they seem, even in the gardening world.

P.S.: One very cold, snowy morning as I swept snow from the brick steps, I looked at my pathetic mum plants. Three of them had frosty blooms covered in snow, but I didn't care. I was now on to pine boughs, pinecones, and wreaths for my holiday decorating. I planned to go shopping later and contemplated buying an evergreen wreath I'd noticed in a sales flyer from my grocery store. However, remembering the Hardy Mum Incident, I quickly headed toward the garden center!

# Tomato Libations

*By Sally Clark*

ometimes you wonder why people do the things they do, until you walk a mile in their shoes or dig a season in their garden.

After my grandparents died, my husband, two children, and I moved into their tiny four-room house in a small town of about five hundred people. My grandfather had always planted his vegetable garden on the east side of the house between the house and the road, barely five feet from a moderately traveled street. I wondered why he didn't plant his garden behind the house, between the apricot trees and the peach orchard, away from the dust and traffic of the road.

Although we were city folk, my husband, Mike, enjoyed working a vegetable garden. As soon as the ground warmed, he cleared and planted the long, sunny rows my grandfather had tended years before.

One day in early spring, Mike cut plastic milk jugs in half and placed them around the young tomato plants to protect them from the spring wind. As Mike worked the garden, Bunny Weinheimer slowed his pickup truck and pulled up next to the chicken wire fence that separated the garden from the road. Bunny was the owner of the local grocery store.

Bunny rolled his truck window down and shook his head. "Don't you city boys know that's not where milk comes from?" he asked with mock concern.

Mike grinned. "Well now, Bunny, you see that row of milk jugs over there? Those are male milk jugs. And you see this row over here? These are female milk jugs. I think it's gonna work." My husband was never one to be outdone.

With a broad laugh, Bunny drove his truck down the road. He licked his finger and stroked it downward in the air, scoring one for the city boy. It seems my grandfather chose his garden space to cultivate friendships as well as produce.

As spring turned into summer, I watched from the kitchen window as other pickup trucks slowed and stopped beside what was now my husband's garden. Every truck seemed to have a beer cooler in the back and a driver who was happy to offer Mike a cold one. To encourage the friendships, Mike stopped working, leaned on whatever rake or hoe was in his hands, and welcomed the conversation. He was a light drinker, so when the pickup pulled out of sight, Mike poured the beer out onto the garden.

Years later, after our children were grown, our son had his own garden. One day, I caught him pouring beer onto his tomato plants.

"What are you doing, Son?" I asked.

"Watering the tomatoes," he answered.

"With beer?"

"Sure . . . that's what Dad did. I thought you were supposed to feed tomatoes beer."

I laughed. "Well, honey, Dad was just trying to grow friends, but I guess it never did the tomatoes any harm."

# Notes from the Huckleberry Goddess

*By Susan Sundwall*

Around about April they start coming back to me—the jars. Usually I get a smile with each one (a big smile) because of a much-desired and hoped-for refill.

"We just loved that strawberry jam," says Kate, my daughter-in-law. "Especially Sam."

She throws that in because our Sam is the cutest kindergartner on the planet. And yes, I'm his grandma.

"That was a great birthday gift," says my best friend with a smile and a wink. This wonderful person boils water well, but not much else. Make jam? Please!

But I'm not stupid, and they don't fool me. I know that they know berry-picking season is not too far off, and they glow with anticipating full jars of strawberry, blueberry, and blackberry jam. Every year I grab my big speckled enamel bucket and head out to the local berry fields to, among other things, fulfill my jam eaters' expectations. I have to admit, I love being needed and admired in such a fashion, but it never occurred to me to grow berries of my own until one year when I overheard two women conversing in the blueberry fields. That's right—I'm a berry field eavesdropper, so shoot me.

Anyway, the conversation went something like this:

"These are so big they remind me of huckleberries; remember those?" said the first woman. She was quite a bit older than me and looked as though she had a good many such remembrances.

"Oh, huckleberries. My mother used to pick them over by the railroad tracks," said her picking companion. "I'd almost forgotten."

"We had huckleberry pie that was out of this world. You don't see them around much anymore. Too bad."

My head was buzzing. Visions of Huckleberry Finn and Huckleberry Hound came to mind, but so did the romance of the whole thing. Wouldn't it be great to be able to offer huckleberry jam to my family and friends? I could just hear them: "Mom, where on earth did you find huckleberries?" "Grandma, this is the best jam ever! Better than strawberry, even."

Oh, the glory of it!

As it happens, the following spring (Ha! What am I saying? It was January!), in the pages of my favorite garden catalog, was an offering of huckleberry plants. Wow, was this a sign that I should give huckleberry planting a shot or what? I read furiously about planting them, all the ways to use them, and how high yielding they were. I ordered some and eagerly anticipated their arrival. Let's see, Huckleberry Queen . . . um . . . or Huckleberry Diva maybe. Well, somehow I would gain glory from these plants. I just knew it. It was in the stars or something.

Soon they arrived and I unpacked the little pots. Didn't look like much, but I've always been a believer in potential, and I got busy. Never had any plants been so cosseted. I took the peat pots, watered them, and set them up in the laundry room, as it was still chilly March. I mother-henned them like crazy, and soon they popped their little heads out and, to my delight, began growing at a phenomenal rate. I wondered briefly why more people didn't grow huckleberries.

When May finally came, I lugged the now hearty plants to the freshly turned garden and entrusted the ground to their care. I trussed them up, laid down that black stuff for weeds, and watched as the days turned to weeks and the blossoms turned to berries, like big grape clusters. Amazing! *Queen,* I was thinking, *Huckleberry Queen.*

So a couple of months passed and the plants and their fruit were gorgeous. I've never had such success. I could have kissed those ladies in the blueberry field.

One morning I rambled up to the garden and decided to sneak a taste. I lifted a cluster from one of the biggest plants and broke it off. Pop! Into my mug they went. They burst full on my tongue and tasted . . . awful! What the devil? My mind refused to consider that huckleberries might not taste good, so I decided they probably weren't ripe. Okay, I'd wait. Surely the taste would improve with exposure to sunlight. The sun makes the sugar in the berries—I knew that. Read it somewhere in a reliable publication. So I waited. A week later they were looking so good on the vine. I imagined myself as a goddess of old descending to gather a toga full to take home to the Sun. Did I hazard another taste? Yup. Any good? Nope. I shook my goddess fist and decided it was time for emergency measures. I called my brother-in-law, the gardener extraordinaire.

"Oh, huckleberries," he said. I clutched my heart. I knew Mr. Knowledge would tell it straight. "I think those need to be cooked before they taste right."

"Really?" I exclaimed, happy like a little kid. "That's what I'd planned to do with them anyway!" What a relief.

Next step: I gathered all those jars from my loyal jam people, harvested my huckleberries, and got my little jam factory going in the kitchen. The fresh-picked berries were gorgeous, and I lavished them with love, sugar, and Certo. A double batch, too. After a few hours of joyful labor, I looked at my newspaper-covered table where the glistening jars of huckleberry jam sat. *The Queen*; I could hear them calling me that. *Or maybe Goddess . . . yeah, Goddess.*

Except I did another hazardly taste of the scrapings from the jam pot, and I gotta tell you, it wasn't good. In fact, it was one of the most awful things I'd ever tasted in my life. My tongue recoiled, and I looked at the glistening jars in dismay. Did I just spend a fortune in time, anticipation, and sugar to create this stuff? 'Fraid so. I could only just bear to think about it. Time for more emergency measures. I resorted to my gang of three to come to my rescue.

First, blame others. Those women in the berry field were only teasing each other. They hated huckleberries. And somebody had conned the garden catalog, too. But worst of all, Mr. Knowledge was blowing smoke. He didn't know a thing about huckleberries!

Second, blame myself. I probably did something wrong, like use the wrong water on them or something. How could I be so stupid?

Third, suck it up and get over it.

Number three is what I wound up doing. I let the jars glisten on the table for a few days more, then I opened them and dumped the jam into my speckled enamel pot. I hauled them outside and dumped the whole mess at the far edges of the yard.

I'm so glad I'd intended to surprise everyone with my wonderful jam and therefore hadn't gloated too much about my attempt to bring the romantic huckleberry into their lives. In fact, Huckleberry Finn and Hound can have 'em! And furthermore, if you pass my yard and happen to see plants poking up where I dumped that jam, feel free to bring your dog along, and he can shoot them down with his water! There's a jar of strawberry jam in it for you.

Yours truly,

The Huckleberry Goddess

# Peanut Troubles

*By Christy Lowman*

ad enjoyed spending time with his father. They shared a lot of the same interests and hobbies and spent a lot of time together throughout the years. Two things they enjoyed were eating peanuts and raising cows. When Dad was a child, he could always be found by Grandpa's side learning farming and gardening techniques. Later in life they formed a farming partnership that was valid until Grandpa died.

I love hearing stories of when my father was a little boy. This particular tale that follows is one that became my all-time favorite.

"One fine May morning when I was a little boy, I was busy following your grandpa down the freshly plowed rows in the garden. That day he was showing me how to plant peanuts. I silently walked in Grandpa's shadow up and down the designated rows. Grandpa's plans were to drop the peanuts on the ground and come back afterward to cover them up. While Grandpa concentrated on laying the peanuts perfectly spaced apart, I kept the questions and conversation short and sweet," Dad smiled, remembering back.

You see, Dad was busy doing other things. Sneaky things.

"As the humidity rose and the sun beat down on the back of our necks, we slowly walked to the end of the last row. When Grandpa turned around to start the covering-up process, he looked in amazement at the ground and then at me.

"He shot me a scowl and said, 'Boy, don't you know that will get you into trouble?'

"I wiped the sweat out of my eyes and said, 'I don't care.'"

I looked at Dad with big eyes of disbelief and asked, "What did you do to make him mad?"

"Amazingly, I managed to pull one over on your grandpa, which was unusual because he didn't miss a thing. I managed to successfully pick up every single peanut without Grandpa noticing. Instead of putting them in my pocket, I ate every last one of them. My belly was so full, I didn't care about the trouble I was getting into."

"So what did you get into trouble for? Sassing or for eating the peanuts?" I giggled.

"Both," he said.

Dad learned other gardening tricks from Grandpa as well, such as "Don't use Sevin Dust on your plants to get rid of those pesky potato bugs!"

"Grandpa used to have each one of us carry a jar of kerosene and go out and pick the potato bugs off the plants one by one and drop them in the jar," Dad said.

"Why?" I asked. "Was he too tight with his money to buy Sevin Dust?"

"Oh no. He had plenty of Sevin Dust out in the shed. This was just one of Grandpa's many creative ways of keeping us busy," Dad said. "You see, Grandpa's number-one philosophy when it came to raising children was to make sure they had plenty of things to do so they wouldn't have any extra time to get into trouble."

Apparently keeping Dad busy by showing him how to plant peanuts failed, but picking potato bugs worked wonderfully!

"Eew, I can't imagine," I gasped. All I could picture was poor bugs swimming around in kerosene!

Dad giggled, "Yep, that was one of the few fun things we got to do."

"I'm so glad you didn't make me do that when I was a kid." I wrinkled up my nose-thinking about the stinky kerosene.

# Pumpkins, Pumpkins, Pumpkins

*By Christy Lowman*

Ever since I was a little girl, I've loved pumpkin patches. Every year, Dad used to take my brother and me to a local pumpkin farm to pick out one to carve for Halloween.

There were pumpkins as far as the eye could see. Every year I had a new size and shape in mind. It was so fun to dodge my way through the patch looking for the perfect one for a jack-o'-lantern.

Dad always grew the old-fashioned pumpkins used solely for baking. He tried his hand at growing a variety of fruits and vegetables in his garden.

"I'm going to be just like Dad and grow pumpkins when I grow up," I said. "Only I'm going to grow all kinds, so kids can come from all around and pick out ones for jack-o'-lanterns at my pumpkin patch."

As I grew older, we quit going to the magical pumpkin patch, but we would always have pumpkins for Halloween and Thanksgiving. The ones meant for Halloween were either carved or had faces painted on them. All of my painted ones had to have freckles.

Dad grew the baking pumpkins especially for Mom—that is,

the pumpkins that the cows didn't eat first. She would bake and scoop the flesh out to make fresh pumpkin pies. There isn't anything better than a homemade pumpkin pie and baked, salted pumpkin seeds to eat!

When I got married, we moved to the air force base where my husband was stationed, and I fell in love with the local "pumpkin patch." It wasn't like any pumpkin patch I had ever been to before. There were all kinds of pumpkins—red, white, and blue ones; ugly ones that looked like they were growing warts; and even petite, striped ones. I was in heaven! A tractor pulled a hayride to the pumpkin patch where you could pick whichever pumpkin type, shape, and size you wanted. It didn't get any better than that. There were also several other activities for the children to do, along with places that served homemade treats.

"This is it!" I exclaimed. "This is what I want to do back home for kids in the neighborhoods where we grew up!"

"Okay," my husband said.

I don't think he quite understood my determination at that point. We would go to this famous pumpkin patch several times each year. The more we went, the more determined I got that this is what I wanted to do back home.

When the time came for us to move back, the first thing we did was look for a place to move to. We decided to buy a nice piece of land, around thirty-two acres, way out in the middle of nowhere and on the top of a mountain.

"This would be perfect for my pumpkin patch," I said, visualizing where I would put what.

"Sure, when we get moved up here, you can have your pumpkin patch," said my husband.

We looked faithfully for a way to build a house on top of our land but just couldn't afford it at the time, so we were forced to look for a reasonable fixer-upper to live in for the time being. The house we settled on was in a small town about forty-five minutes away from the land. I still had the desire to have my pumpkin patch, but each year we lived there, it would dwindle some.

Five years after we bought the land, our first child was born, and I got the urge to have jack-o'-lanterns again. One of my clients at the bank gave me two pumpkins. Both were cooking pumpkins, but one was the perfect round shape to become a jack-o'-lantern. I had plans to make the other one into pies, just like the ones Mom made.

Though my intentions were good, the pumpkins started to rot before I got a chance to do anything with them, just like so many other projects I had in mind to do.

"I'm going to throw these out in the ditch," my husband said one autumn evening when we were cleaning off the porch.

We have a large ditch that runs along the side of our property that carries all the runoff water from the street to the creek in the back. The ditch is hideous and ends up full of whatever trash people throw out. However, the weeds grow great, and it is home to thousands of mosquitoes.

The next summer rolled around and plants started to grow in the ditch—except this time, they weren't weeds but pumpkin plants!

We were in a severe drought all summer; the grass was brown and dead, but my pumpkin plants and pumpkins thrived!

"I'm so tired of trying to mow around pumpkins and pumpkin vines," my husband would complain.

The only grass that grew in the yard was around the ditch, due to the minimum rain.

"Don't you dare touch them," I threatened. "I'm finally getting to grow my mini pumpkin patch."

My husband only threw out two different kinds of pumpkins, but we ended up with three different species. We had candy roasters, small round pumpkins, and a third that was a mixture of the two.

"Those aren't pumpkins, they're gourds," corrected my mother-in-law.

"Nope, they're 100 percent pumpkin," I said. "They are old-timey ones; that's why their flesh is skin-colored instead of the bright orange."

That was one thing nobody was going to argue with me about. I knew my pumpkins!

Everybody enjoyed watching them grow. My brother would make his weekly visit to come over and admire them. He even did the honors of gathering them.

"You need to set a sign out at the road that says 'Organic Pumpkins for Sale,'" my brother suggested. "They haven't had any pesticides or anything done to them."

"I would be scared to eat those," said my husband. "Who knows what they have been in contact with in that ditch."

I was just proud to have grown them (what little I did), that I gave them away to whoever was brave enough to want to cook or carve them.

"Those are the best pies I have ever made," commented my neighbor. "If you have any extra, I'll take some more to freeze."

I made a few pies, along with a few other brave souls, and was impressed. You could not have asked for a better pumpkin. These had more meat and fewer seeds and strings than any I'd ever seen.

I thought I would have around a dozen pumpkins altogether but ended up with close to seventy-five! I had them coming out of my ears. Half of the porch was covered in different shapes and sizes, but that was okay—I was in heaven!

When frost came around, whatever was left that no one wanted went to feed my dad's cows, and boy, did they enjoy them! There were a few that ended up rotting. When I picked them up and paused, I guess my husband read my mind.

"Don't even think about it. Don't throw any more pumpkins into that ditch," he said. "Next year I want to be able to mow in a straight line," he laughed.

Secretly, when he wasn't looking I threw two in there, but to his advantage nothing came of it the next year.

So now I'm content, but it won't be long before I start dreaming of my mega pumpkin patch again, so my kids and other kids can come from miles around to pick their favorite one for their very own jack-o'-lantern!

# Critters in the
# Garden

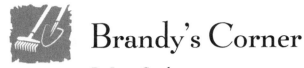

# Brandy's Corner

*By Joyce Stark*

t wasn't until we reached our fifties that we found time enough to concentrate a bit more on our small garden in our home in northeast Scotland. As neither my husband Eric nor I knew very much about the subject, we decided to start cautiously. We planted some snowdrop bulbs in a row outside our hall window. Eric was just putting the last bulb in when he glanced down the row and saw Brandy, our ginger-colored cat, sitting on top of the first bulb planted. He was about to shoo him away when, in the cold air, he saw steam emerging from beneath Brandy and realized he had fully utilized the loose earth—cat-style!

We got that sorted out and went to bed satisfied that our gardening days had begun. Next morning we got up and three of the snowdrop bulbs were scattered about in the garden. Brandy had made an early morning visit and decided these little round things were toys we had planted for him to play with!

No amount of "shooing" could persuade Brandy away from this idea, and a series of crocus bulbs, salad onions, and other assorted bulbs failed to remain in the ground. Eric had a brainwave that planting bulbs in that area was not a good idea! We are both of the opinion that any animal is part of the family. We felt that as this was also Brandy's garden, and he continually climbed the trees and played in the garden, we would have to work around this problem. We put a young shrub in the corner that a knowledgeable neighbor had told us would grow quickly and could withstand anything. It grew okay, but it couldn't withstand Brandy's spraying, so within its first year, the poor shrub gave up the ghost, and Brandy went back to digging in "his corner" of the garden.

As we got more proficient, we had a good show of spring and summer flowers, but no matter what we did, Brandy's corner remained taboo. We did finally get a few chives to grow close to it, but that was all he would allow. Brandy was a gentle, sweet-natured cat, and although we called him a ginger-colored cat, sometimes he looked almost pink, and because of that everyone knew him.

No matter how many plants and shrubs we put in the garden, he never touched any of them. He dug around them, played around them, even slept underneath some of them, as long as "his corner" was kept vacant. It was strange, but nearly every time we planted anything, weeded, or just turned over the soil, he would appear out of nowhere. Our neighbor laughed and said it looked as if he was just making sure that we didn't put anything in his corner. Sometimes he even sat in the corner cleaning or watching us, just to make it clear we shouldn't get any more ideas about it.

Brandy was seventeen when, after a short illness, he finally passed away last year. We were devastated, but knew exactly where we were going to bury him—in his special corner. We wrapped him in his favorite blanket and put him to rest in his corner and vowed that no matter what, we would never plant anything there. That was in the winter, and strangely enough, when we were weeding during the following spring, we noticed something growing in the corner that wasn't just another weed. We asked our neighbor to take a look, and she said to let it grow a little so she could identify what it was. As it grew, it was clear that it was a shrub, and we were tempted just to pull it out, but to us that was destroying a living thing, and something made us leave it alone.

As it grew a bit more and very quickly, our neighbor identified it as what we call "broom" in Scotland; it grows abundantly on our golf courses and has pretty yellow flowers. We were about to suggest we dig it up and offer it to a friend when our neighbor shook her head. "It's not just ordinary broom; it looks like what I know as 'decorative broom' that is very unusual. If it comes to full bloom, it is really beautiful, with an unusual pinky/peachy-colored flower."

Once we were alone, I looked at Eric and asked, "Do you think it's odd that in the spot where Brandy is buried, an unusual plant has appeared with much the same coloring as he was?"

The question was enough. We left the plant alone, and that summer it had few flowers but was a pretty young plant. This year it was amazing—a mass of beautiful flowers—that outshone anything else in our modest garden. We couldn't have put a more fitting tribute to our lost friend in "his corner" if we had tried.

It can be explained away easily enough as something the birds gifted to our garden, however unusual the plant might be, but that's not what I believe. A garden is not just a place for pretty flowers, but it is something to share. We shared it with Brandy, and to me, the bush is an acknowledgment of that and his way of thanking us and still sharing the garden with us.

# The Vegetable Garden

*By Nancy Baker*

"You know what I'd like to do?" my husband Ted asked.

"What?" I responded with some trepidation. The last time he asked such a question, we had gone sailing in a borrowed boat—for all of two minutes. The wind changed directions, but we didn't. It takes a relatively short time to capsize. On the other hand, it takes an extremely long time to right the boat, especially when the first mate (me) is more interested in what might be lurking beneath the surface of the murky saltwater we were in than in flipping the boat.

"Plant a vegetable garden."

"Huh?"

"A vegetable garden. We always had one when I was a kid. I can still taste those scrumptious tomatoes right off the vine. And the corn—so sweet you'd think it was buried in sugar instead of soil." Ted was on a roll describing all of his favorite vegetables.

"But you lived in the country. We live in a subdivision."

"Our backyard is big enough. And we could get the kids involved. It could be a family project." Ted knew how to get me.

I was always trying to think of ways to do things as a family.

I have to admit, much to my surprise, our kids took to the idea like ducks to water. Our teenage boys loved the thought of "destroying" our backyard (less to mow) with a tiller, much in the fashion of *Tim the Tool Man*. Ted and the boys laid out the garden precisely using stakes and string, while my ten-year-old daughter, Laura, and I watched our backyard shrink to half its size.

The next step was to fence it. Our two dogs would never be able to tell the difference between play (and poop) ground and the vegetable garden. The fencing was accomplished with engineering accuracy.

Then it was Laura's and my turn.

"What are we planting now, Mom?"

"Okra. It grows tall, so we'll plant it near the back."

"Then what?"

"Corn. It grows tall too. Then tomatoes. We'll have to stake them. Then peppers—bell and jalapeños. Some squash and maybe eggplant."

"Ugh!"

"Okay, maybe not."

"Hey, Mom. Didn't Pat pick okra for Mr. Cangelosi last summer?"

"Yeah."

"Didn't he say it was all sticky and made him itch?"

"Yeah."

"Well, I don't want to pick it."

"Me neither. Pat should pick it since he has experience."

"Yeah!" The grin on Laura's face was as wide as the Mississippi River. We both sat back on our heels, laughing at the thought.

The garden flourished, and although weeding was not the favorite part for any of us, the nightly discussions at the dinner table about the progress of the various crops was a welcome change from the bickering that had accompanied the meal previously. I'll never forget the first tomato, carefully cut into five pieces, salted and peppered, and then savored—all one bite of it.

The corn produced enough ears for one whole meal. The peppers, on the other hand, wouldn't quit producing. My favorite, the squash, got worms and went kaput. The okra produced steadily and had to be picked every day. There are only so many ways you can fix okra, so my neighbors became the recipients of our daily take.

Ted was right about one thing. Tomatoes are the best right off the vine. Laura skipped out the back door to pick some for our evening meal and came running back in screaming, "A snake! Mom, there's a snake in our garden."

Ted dropped the newspaper and headed for the shed. "I'll get him." He reappeared, hoe in hand. "Where . . . where is he, baby?"

By this time Pat and Vince were in on the hunt.

"Where'd you see him, Laura?"

"By the peppers," she called, balancing herself high on a lawn chair.

The dogs by now knew something was up and were barking, running up and down the fence line.

"Maybe he crawled over by the corn." Pat tromped right over the okra and pushed the cornstalks aside.

"Nope, maybe he's under the dead squash plants." Vince made a dash for them, uprooting several hot bells as he went.

"I've got him," Ted yelled. He triumphantly held up the limp snake, draped over the end of the hoe. "See the dead snake." Ted waved the reptile at the dogs, who responded with yips, jumping as high as Ted held the snake.

"Look how long he is," Vince exclaimed.

"He's so gross," Laura said. I agreed.

"I'll get the trash can," Pat offered.

Ted dumped the snake in the trash can and then surveyed the garden. "Demolished" is the word that came to mind. Laura began to cry, whether from fear of the snake or from the demise of our garden, I'm not sure.

"Don't cry, honey," Ted comforted. "Our garden had a good run."

"Yeah," Vince joined in, "and, what a finale—a snake hunt."

"Besides, no more okra to pick." Pat's smile was ear to ear.

Monday morning. Trash day. "Vince," I hollered, "I'm taking the kitchen garbage out. Will you take the can to the front?"

"Okay."

I was busily planning my day as I lifted the trash can lid.

"Hisssssssss!"

"Ohmygosh! That #$%^&* snake is still alive!" I dropped the garbage bag, slapped the lid back on the trash can, and did what any red-blooded American woman would do: I called my husband. "Ted, you'd better come kill that sorry snake you already killed." Turns out it was a hognose snake, and they are notorious for playing possum when they're disturbed. I never did know what Ted did to him.

Several weeks passed and the vegetable garden looked pretty

pathetic. Then the rains came, unheard of in South Texas in August. Three straight days of unrelenting rain. Our garden was a mud hole.

The day the sun finally peeked out, Pat brought his girlfriend, Maria, for a visit. He vividly recounted the infamous snake chase, showing her the exact locations of the search and final demise of the hognose. The fence sagged, and he carefully helped her over so that he could precisely describe the event. She lost her shoe in the muck. Pat bent over to retrieve it. She slipped and accidentally pushed him face-first into the mud. He turned and pulled her down with him. Thus began the infamous mud brawl. It was the beginning of a lifelong relationship (Maria later became our daughter-in-law) and the end of the vegetable garden.

Some gardens produce beautiful flowers, others prizewinning vegetables, still others provide a place for quiet reverie. Ours produced family memories that always bring smiles to our faces. "Remember that time in the vegetable garden when . . ."

Author's note: Snakes are actually good for the garden because they eat many critters that like to eat your plants, including insects, slugs, snails, mice, and voles. So, unless they are poisonous and a direct threat, you should consider leaving those snakes alone.

# Mr. Chipmunk

*By Nancy Edwards Johnson*

Freshly awakened from his winter nap, Mr. Chipmunk scurried onto our deck. With a lightning flick of his striped brown tail, he checked his surroundings and vanished under a bed of hostas.

In a few days, his shyness will vanish and he'll be up to his old tricks, running the deck railings and popping his soft, fuzzy head from beneath the pansies. After knowing him for years, I've caught on to most of his shenanigans. I love watching him maneuver and gladly go along with his games.

Last year, when the creeping phlox spread its colorful blooms over the rocks lining the edge of the garden, a rabbit moved in to take his meals. Not wanting to wish bad things on the bunny and unhappy at the loss of our phlox, I asked my dad to make me an old-timey wooden rabbit gum. I'd catch the bunny and deposit him in a grassy meadow to munch on clover instead of my flower blooms.

The first morning after I baited the trap, I found it sprung. Light movement and scratching came from within. Carefully, so as not to startle the bunny, my daughter Jennifer eased open the

door. To our surprise, two shiny black eyes sparkled back at us—
Mr. Chipmunk.

Jennifer begged to keep him to tame for a pet, but at my insis-
tence, she turned him loose. He scurried a few feet away, and then
stopped in his furry little tracks to squeal his displeasure at us. I
reset the rabbit gum.

Five minutes later, the chipmunk was back. He crept around
the wooden gum, curious as a cat. Finally, he jumped on top,
examining the trapping mechanism. In less than ten minutes,
he'd figured out how to spring the trap.

The first slam scared him silly, and he sat on the trap, squealing wildly. I walked close to him and he scattered, only to return
shortly to spring the reset trap. A slave to his fascination and a
slow learner, Mr. Chipmunk spent most of that day trapped in the
rabbit gum.

The next morning started off busy, with mowing to do and
flower beds to mulch. No one noticed the door to the rabbit gum
was closed once again. Shortly, we heard frantic chattering coming from the yard. An angry ball of fluff came dashing across the
grass, squealing his heart out. He raced a few feet away from the
deck and fluttered around in circles, alternately chattering and
squeaking and then disappearing under the safety of the hosta
leaves.

Finally, I noticed the sprung rabbit gum. Once more, Jennifer
slid open the door and peeked inside. *Hmm, it's another chipmunk.*
So we have at least two, and I've always heard that there's no such
thing as two chipmunks.

Over the years we've learned that our chipmunks love peanuts.

Judging by the amount they'll carry off in a day, they all do. Never knowing how many chipmunks we're feeding, we put out plenty.

We hooked our first Mr. Chipmunk with peanuts a few years back, when some accidentally spilled on the deck. Soon we spotted our little striped friend dashing around to gather them. After that we left a few under the edge of the patio each night and by morning they'd be gone. We started slipping the peanuts closer to the picnic table each day until he was coming for them with us watching. Then we started leaving one peanut instead of a few.

Last summer, each time a peanut vanished we'd drop another. In no time at all, he started making frequent trips to the table, begging for a peanut. He'd grab it and scurry away, running like a streak. Eventually we noticed him sliding through a crack to bury his treasure underneath the patio. He'd flatten himself paper-thin and off he'd go.

One day, he tried to maneuver the crack with his peanut held vertically in his mouth, and he bumped against the stones. We laughed watching him until he figured out his problem and turned the peanut around. Carrying it horizontally, he then glided gracefully into the crack and disappeared from sight.

In our innocence, we thought he was eating all the peanuts. Then distinctive oval-shaped leaves began to appear among the ferns and ivies of our planters, and we learned what he was really doing with them. But everybody needs a little gardening spot somewhere, including Mr. Chipmunk.

Last year as chilly weather brought our gardening season to a close, we planted a huge bed of salad onion sets, anticipating green onions in early spring. Shortly the onions were out of the soil and scattered over the gravel of the driveway. I retrieved and replanted them, totally mystified as to what would dig up onions, of all things. Right. Mr. Chipmunk.

This spring we have garden onions sprouting in the driveway, on the hill behind the house, and in all the baskets and planters growing under our deck. Mr. Chipmunk had such a time doing his planting that he's led us to believe that he doesn't hibernate the entire winter.

When visitors come and sit on our deck and notice a tiny brown streak moving among the flowers, they can count themselves lucky, because our furry friend doesn't come out for everyone. Sometimes he'll vanish for a week. But he always returns, begging for peanuts or to show off a new trick. He's a proven beggar and a thief. He rearranges our plantings, and he plants his own garden in disagreeable places. But he's a clown to watch, and I wouldn't want to face a planting season without him.

# Christmas in July

*By Nancy Gibbs*

**Y**ou never know what you're going to see way down deep in southern Georgia. One summer, Papa, my father-in-law, planted his annual garden next to a busy highway. He had dozens of rows of peas, corn, and tomatoes.

To his dismay, however, many small animals ate his vegetables while he wasn't looking. A scarecrow worked rather well at keeping the crows away by day, but when the sun went down, apparently he slept with the rest of us. The raccoons made a feast of Papa's garden delicacies.

After getting aggravated with the culprit raccoons, Papa ran an extension cord out to the garden and hooked up a radio. For several nights the critters stayed away as the music played by the light of the moon. Unfortunately, they became familiar with the sounds that the radio made and soon began to make their nightly raids again. Papa was furious.

One day when he went to get his hoe and shovel, he spied a five-foot-tall, lighted Santa Claus in the back of the utility house and an idea was born. Papa pulled Saint Nick out, dusted him off, and sat him on a cinder block in the middle of the garden, facing the highway. Santa ruled over the tomatoes and corn. He kept an eye out for the peas, as he shown brightly in the garden. Instead of speeding by, many drivers drove by slowly and some even stopped to admire Santa Claus as he stood guard over the vegetables.

There's nothing like the spirit of Christmas being shared in July to get attention, not only from the neighbors, but also from hungry nighttime critters. While the neighbors laughed, the small critters were petrified.

The raccoons never came back. Papa's crops thrived, and we are still enjoying the frozen vegetables that Santa so diligently watched over last July. Unfortunately, old Saint Nick didn't help Papa "hoe, hoe, hoe" his garden, but he lightened up many people's lives as he stood proudly facing the highway in the middle of July.

Next July, Papa plans to play Christmas music as well.

# Planting Memories

*By Anita E. Machek*

"Gardens should be filled with memories, just like our lives." I rubbed Belle's neck as she stuck her nose into my apron pocket. "We'll make some new ones here, you and I." Belle is my new gardening partner, a golden retriever who came to us after being abandoned following Hurricane Rita, which had blown through my garden, leaving it and my home in ruins.

Many of the plants that had held memories of my life were gone, either because of the storm or the clearing that had to be done when the old house was razed to make room for a new house. The hundred-foot pines that had been there from the beginning were gone. Crepe myrtles I received as birthday gifts from my children were destroyed, and all but two of my precious flower beds were wrecked. Over the years other plants and memories had gone as well. Only one of two sweet gum trees remained, one having come down in a storm the morning my husband passed away. Plants leave the garden for one reason or another and are replaced by new ones.

I looked at the two remaining flower beds, and memories flooded my mind. Bright red Saint Joseph's lilies with a story all their own: "These were Granny and Blackie's lilies."

I sat on the bench and began to tell Belle the story. "Granny gave me two bulbs from her yard just before she passed away, and I planted them over in the bed by the mimosa trees. They are gone now too. Blackie, a Labrador, was my gardening friend then, and she watched me while I planted them that fall. The next spring I watched for them to come up but never did see them. Then one day that summer I saw these bright red lilies blooming in the middle of the lawn. I couldn't figure it out. How did they get there? I carefully dug them and moved them back to their place in the bed.

"Later that day, I saw Blackie through the kitchen window just as carefully digging them up. She carried them to another spot and dug a hole, put them in, and gently used her nose to cover them with dirt. I thought, My goodness—what is wrong with that dog? I promptly went out and moved them again, only to have Blackie once again move the bulbs. I made the decision right then and there: a new bed was being made right where Blackie had put the bulbs, and that is where they are now. When she died we buried her there by the lilies."

Belle looked at me and then at the multitude of flowers.

"The amaryllis came from that crotchety old lady up on the hill; she always pretended to be meaner than she really was." She nuzzled my hand, and I rubbed her neck again.

"Let's plant something," I said. She let out a little yip as if in agreement.

Belle helped as I dug, pushing dirt back into the hole with her nose. We planted a gardenia I started from a cutting the preacher's wife gave to me. Each time I see it bloom in my garden, I will remember her, and Belle helping me plant it.

Since that day Belle and I, with some help from grandchildren, have begun a blue and white butterfly garden to remember other pets that have gone on before us. We have planted roses to commemorate special days, as well as ferns where the frogs and crickets like to gather at night.

Belle and I continue to make memories in our garden; the latest is Belle's lettuce bed. I planted nice, neat rows, and as soon as I went into the house, she began to dig and scatter the seed. It is the prettiest leaf lettuce I have ever grown, and Belle helps herself to a leaf or two whenever she likes.

# Dusting the Beans

*By Michelle Close Mills*

I once saw a TV show where the heroine was a little girl who owned a potted lemon tree. She fussed over it, talked to it, and even had a specially designed watering can with the tree's name on it. In my twelve-year-old mind, I thought she was a pretty cool kid . . . a real maverick. No dogs and parakeets for her. She had a plant. By golly, I wanted a plant too.

My green-thumbed grandma was tickled pink to learn of my interest. She raided her greenhouse and came up with a pretty button fern, a potted shamrock, two African violets, a peace lily, and a lavender gloxinia to get me started.

My new hobby soon became an obsession. I borrowed books from the library and read up on each variety, then propagated, repotted, and fertilized until my bedroom was overflowing.

"Michelle Lynette Close, entering your room is like tiptoeing through a minefield," Mom complained after accidentally knocking over a freshly watered ficus. "No more plants!"

Okay, I admit things had gotten a wee bit out of hand, but restricting my creativity was like taking away Monet's oil paints. Thankfully, a bigger canvas lay just beyond the patio door.

A longtime loather of yard work, Dad was euphoric when I asked if he needed help with gardening chores. Each day when I got home from school, I'd throw on old clothes and start working in the yard. Our elderly neighbor Mr. Cart, who could never remember my first name, dubbed me "that strange little Close kid who digs in the dirt." Before long my landscaping projects were the talk of our street.

Yet, there remained another frontier to be conquered, the ultimate test of gardeners everywhere: I wanted to grow vegetables. I figured it would be no sweat, having been reared at Grandma's knee, the Muhammad Ali of self-grown produce. She could casually drop a few seeds into the ground and end up with blockbuster yields capable of feeding third-world nations.

However, growing veggies was a trickier task in west central Florida due to the sandy nature of the soil. And I was planting late in the season, when the weather was hot. Even Grandma tried to talk me into planting in the fall. But stubborn as I was, little things like bad dirt and soaring temperatures weren't going to deter me. I even cajoled Dad into helping me clear a small patch out back.

"So what are you planting?" Dad inquired, huffing and puffing as we furiously worked our spades through the sod.

"Green beans," I replied.

"That's it? No tomatoes, onions, or cucumbers?"

"Yes, Daddy, that's it. I love green beans."

He stopped midshovel and gawked at me, sweat drizzling into his eyes.

"Do you mean to tell me that I'm working myself to death on

a Saturday afternoon for a few handfuls of green beans!!?? I don't even like green beans!!" he roared.

Yikes! You'd think I'd suggested planting cannabis.

Soon afterward little heads popped through the soil. As I surveyed my thriving crop, I figured that when we returned from Indiana, the beans would be ready to pick. I couldn't wait.

The night before we left for Grandma and Grandpa's house, I drifted off to sleep, blissfully unaware that a vile assortment of anvil-jawed critters possessing Herculean appetites brazenly plundered my garden as if it were an all-you-could-eat salad bar.

When I discovered the damage the following morning, the bean plants looked as though the U.S. Air Force had used them for target practice. Choking back rising panic, I squeamishly began plucking them off one by one. But after smooshing a dozen or so, I realized I was seriously outnumbered.

Just then Dad honked the horn; it was time to leave for Indiana. I had no choice but to abandon my crop to the elements. For an ambitious young gardener, defeat was a bitter pill. Even worse was what waited at the end of our journey—Grandma's amazing garden, something I could only dream about.

Dread was an alien emotion when it came to visiting my grandparents' home. A kid-friendly place, it smelled of cookies, cloves, noodles, and clean things. There was a squeaky front porch swing, huge maple trees surrounding the grounds, an apple orchard, and beautiful rose beds. And Grandma was there, my best friend.

Grandpa was a different story. He did little more than sit around and look grumpy, so quiet it was easy to forget he was in the house. One of Grandma's lady friends from church didn't see him parked in his chair and accidentally sat on his lap. The only times I heard his voice were when he thundered at my cousins and me for playing too loud, or he asked for the apple butter at dinner. Otherwise, he seldom uttered a peep. If I said hello to him, he'd sometimes grunt in response. More often than not he wouldn't.

Until I made the unconscious blunder of waking him up.

From the time I was small, I talked in my sleep. Mom once heard me contentedly humming "Puff the Magic Dragon" at 2:00 AM. Dad laughed so hard after overhearing me bungle the alphabet as I slept that he stubbed his big toe on the bathroom door. And my subconscious ramblings were a bona fide hit at slumber parties. Everyone thought it was funny.

Everyone except Grandpa.

"Are you all right this morning?" he growled.

"Yes, why do you ask?"

"Last night you woke me up twice because you were hollering at somebody. I'll thank you to remember that an old man needs his sleep!"

Friendship with Grandpa seemed a lost cause.

At least there was Grandma. She wouldn't have cared if I woke her up. However, she deserved better company than the sullen granddaughter who sat miserably on the back porch steps while she tended to healthy crops, a granddaughter too ashamed to admit how badly her first vegetable garden had failed.

Frustrated and jealous, I stomped into the house and flopped down on the couch, ready to bawl my eyes out.

Grandpa glowered at me from his easy chair.

"What's wrong with you?" he asked in a rusty voice.

"Grandpa, do you know anything about growing green beans?" I demanded.

His eyes opened wide with surprise, and he slowly cleared his throat.

"What do you want to know?"

"My green bean garden at home is being eaten by bugs and worms, and I don't know what to do to stop them."

"You have to dust them. Did you do that yet?" Grandpa asked.

I pondered his question for a moment.

"No . . . I didn't think cleaning them would help. But if you say so, I will dust them as soon as I get back."

For a few seconds there was silence.

Then . . . Grandpa laughed.

It started off slow at first, no doubt due to lack of practice, but the dam quickly burst and tears poured down his wrinkled cheeks. I couldn't for the life of me figure out what was so funny, but I was delighted to see him laugh and joined in the fun. Mom and Grandma peered around the corner, bug-eyed in disbelief.

When he smiled a big, toothless grin at me (his teeth were soaking upstairs), I realized that he wasn't as grumpy as I'd believed.

"I thought you didn't like me, Grandpa," I confided.

"Shows how much you know," he chuckled, patting my knee.

It was a day of discoveries . . . and blessings.

The mystery of how to get rid of destructive vermin on future crops was solved, although it was too late to save the current harvest. Oh well. I could always replant in the fall. And if the little buggers returned for a second go at my garden, I'd be armed and ready to dust the heck out of them.

Grandma said that God worked in mysterious ways. How true. I later learned that Grandpa's reclusive behavior was a result of severe depression, something he'd battled for decades. After the green bean debacle, I became one of the few who could perk him up. During my frequent visits, he and I would prattle for hours about Farmer's Almanac predictions, world events, my most recent gardening adventures, and memories of career and family. Grandma said he'd mark off days on the calendar until my next visit. He wasn't the only one.

Who would've thought?

Before he passed away, he made Grandma promise to look after "his little girl." Years later I still smile through tears as I remember how our unlikely friendship began; the most precious of gifts purchased for the low, low price of a small, pest-riddled green bean garden.

Somehow it seemed a pretty fair deal.

# The Object
# of Our Affection

*By Janie Dempsey Watts*

After the death of our beloved Chihuahua, our family found ourselves without a pet for the first time in years. Still grieving, we all felt it was too soon to get another dog, yet we missed the little guy. Without "Chi," I had a handy excuse to skip my daily walk. My husband missed having the dog in his lap as second-in-command on the remote control. And our son Jack had taken to luring "stray" cats in through the back door. It was time to take action. We needed something to take care of besides ourselves, something to nurture.

Flowers might work, at least temporarily. I set off for the nursery to buy seedlings to plant in pots. Jack came along to carry the large bag of potting soil, or so I thought. While browsing the marigolds and petunias, he slipped away. I found him at the checkout counter deep in conversation with a nurseryman and cradling a small plant.

"How often do I water it?" he asked. When had he taken such an interest in plants? But it wasn't just any plant. It was a Venus flytrap, the carnivorous plant that traps and eats insects—the perfect blend of pet and freak. We bought the plant.

Back at home, Jack hovered over the Venus flytrap like a father over a new baby. Every morning he moved the plant to the backyard and measured distilled water into the saucer under the pot. He studied the exact location on the lawn where flies might land. I was brought out for a second opinion, and finally we found a damp spot where tiny gnats sometimes gathered. He left his new darling outdoors all day until dusk when he brought it in from the chill. Several days passed without "Venus" catching any prey. Her leaves were wide open like a butterfly's wings. Concerned, Jack decided to transplant his baby into a larger pot. With my vast horticulture knowledge, I was to perform the operation.

The next morning found us in the garden shed perusing over spare pots and potting soils. He dragged out a big bag of soil and left me to do the dirty work while he logged on to the Internet to learn more about our new plant. It didn't take long to move the plant into a larger pot with dark loamy soil. I was watering it from the garden hose when I heard Jack's voice.

"Have you done it yet? I just found out that's not the right type of soil. Did you use the distilled water?"

"Oops," I said.

"You've killed it—you plant assassin," he said.

"Here—you deal with it," I said, handing him the plant.

"Plant assassin," he muttered as I went back inside. I turned around to see a big grin on his face, and we both laughed. After he had set the plant down to recuperate from its close call with eternity, we returned to the nursery to buy the right soil type. Jack discussed pH balances with the nurseryman.

"It's sphagnum moss, and it has to be in the range of 4.0 to 4.5,"

Jack insisted. I hadn't seen him this interested in science since his sixth-grade "Hooked on Hydraulics" project. As he and the nurseryman talked dirt, I reflected on our Venus flytrap. This delicate-looking carnivorous plant had somehow managed to become our replacement pet.

Sure, we couldn't cuddle with it, but it had distinct advantages over a Chihuahua. Like the Parisians who carry their dogs everywhere, we too could now take our pet to grocery stores and even restaurants. At our favorite outdoor café, Venus might even come in handy, considering the flies that sometimes appeared plateside begging for food. Other unique benefits? There would be no exorbitant vet bills or marked furniture.

When we got home, Jack opened the bag of moss. I removed the "wrong" dirt, replaced it with the correct type, and carefully patted down soil around the plant's thin stem. While I held the pot in my hands, Jack poured a slight stream of distilled water into the saucer where the pot would rest. Seeing my son gently place our Venus onto the saucer, I felt satisfied. The plant somehow looked healthier, thanks to our joint efforts. I stared at its delicate, slightly rose-colored inner leaves and felt something warm and familiar in my chest. A tenderness, I realized, the kind that comes from nurturing someone, or something, other than yourself. Our two-and-a-half-inch new pet hadn't caught a single insect, yet it had successfully captured us.

# Garden
# Transformations

# Barry and the English Garden

*By Harriet Cooper*

I just spent an hour outside admiring my backyard. Like a phoenix rising from its ashes, my English-style garden has risen from what used to be an overgrown bed of weeds.

The metamorphosis began a year ago when Barry, who lives across the street, showed me his garden. He had transformed a paved parking spot at the back of his house into a jewel. Lush flower beds surrounded a calm sea of grass, with two islands of vegetable plants in the middle.

The garden was exquisite. Lust and envy welled up in my heart, and the kernel of an idea took root in my mind. I thanked Barry for showing me his treasure and went home to ruminate.

A few weeks after my tour of his garden, I spied Barry outside working on his front steps. I went over and chatted, once more complimenting him on his garden. As an aside, I said that now that he was finished with his garden, he could flex his muscle and imagination on my backyard. He smiled.

For the next year, every month or so I'd mention my backyard, telling him how much it needed his help. He continued to smile.

One day he said he'd do it. I jumped at the offer and hustled him across the street to show him what he had to work with. He turned pale when he saw the degree of neglect. Then he nodded to himself, as if he could see beyond the mess to something quite beautiful. We came up with a budget, and I handed him a wad of cash.

He planned to buy the earth and some plants early in the season and park them in my backyard. My job was to water the plants. I found out later he kept the most delicate plants in his house because he didn't trust me to keep up my end of the bargain. I did water the plants, when I remembered. None of them died, though a few looked more than a bit wilted. I guess he knew me better than I thought.

We left the work schedule flexible—sometime in July when school was over.

Every so often I'd look out my back window and see more bags of earth or pots of plants arrive. One morning in July, I looked out the window and saw that Barry had arrived. I threw on some clothes and dashed outside. He stood in the backyard muttering, "I thought the yard was smaller."

I flashed him my brightest smile. "So, where do we start?"

For a minute, he looked like an animal caught in the headlights of an oncoming car. Then he girded his loins, or whatever gardeners gird when they're about to attack five years of neglected lawn and flower beds, and pointed to a particularly dense patch of weeds.

Two days later, the weeds were gone. I was tempted to take a congratulatory nap. Barry, however, was made of sterner stuff. Unrolling landscaper's weed block plastic, he laid out the paths bordering the flower beds. The previous year, when the idea to work on my backyard had taken root, I did something very smart. Well, I did two smart things: (1) I enlisted Barry, and (2) when I had my front pad parking redone, I had the old pavers moved to a corner of my backyard. The stones were going to be reborn as decorative borders.

While Barry leveled and placed, I fetched and carried. A few hours later, the first of the beds was outlined. The next day, Barry fashioned a graceful curve around my tree, balanced by a small curve on the other side. An English garden had taken its first step from his imagination to my reality.

The following day we headed out to buy more flowers and gardening supplies. We grabbed a huge, two-tiered flatbed cart and roamed tables and metal shelves looking for plants. It didn't take long to fill the cart. Alyssum montanum. Scabiosa columbaria. Coreopsis auriculata. Armeria maritima. Dianthus deltoides. Achillea. Physostegia virginiana. Shirobana spirea. Even the names sounded wonderful. Then we headed for the more prosaic necessities. Mulch. Topsoil. Manure. Luckily, Barry's midsize car put a limit on our enthusiasm. If not, we probably would have bought out the entire nursery.

During day four, Barry extended the borders of two existing flower beds while I continued to fetch pavers. Then the planting began. He carefully mixed in manure and topsoil for each plant while I followed behind and added mulch, one handful at a time, under his watchful eye.

By that evening, the garden had revealed more of its final shape. Neighbors on both sides who had previously wanted to report me to the Garden Police for cruel and unusual punishment to plant life came to ooh and aah.

Six more days of work ensued. Trying to figure out the perfect shape of the central bed consumed Barry. His original circle diminished to an oval and from there to an elongated oblong that flared at the bottom. Unfortunately, rectangular pavers refused to give him the corners he wanted.

Determination, careful planning, and plants with large leaves combined to take the harsh edges off the corners. The final plants went in. To give the garden year-round appeal, Barry reserved part of this central bed for evergreens. Bushes formed the backbone of the bed, with more delicate perennials fanning out to form the ribs. As usual, I followed two steps behind with the mulch—a disciple learning at the feet of the master.

The only thing left was filling the pathways with small stones. A landscaping company delivered a cubic yard of pea gravel in front of my house. Countless wheelbarrow trips later, the pea gravel was transferred to the backyard. Four hours later, Barry raked and leveled the last of the stones and strategically placed four mosaic stepping-stones to add a final burst of color to the pathways.

The garden was finished.

While Barry was deservedly pleased with the result, I was speechless in amazement at the transformation. Although I had been collecting gardening books for years, I treated them as I treated my home decorating books and cookbooks—more fiction than fact. I'd page through the books, admiring the beautiful gardens, never expecting to have any of them.

Now I do. I am in love with my garden. Even as I type this, more slowly than usual since my fingers remain stiff and swollen from weeding, mulching, and hauling pavers, I peek outside my office window that looks onto my garden. My gaze dances from one flower bed to the other, noting the frilly leaves on one plant, the tall, slim shoots on another. I watch the tiger lilies sway in the breeze and the smaller plants hug the earth. Butterflies float from one flower to another, adding more grace and charm to my garden.

Then I remember my promise to Barry: to water, weed, and care for my garden. I tell myself that's an easy promise to keep, as the garden invites me to come and play in it. Besides, if I slack off, Barry will kill me . . . and he knows where I live.

# READER/CUSTOMER CARE SURVEY

We care about your opinions! Please take a moment to fill out our online Reader Survey at **http://survey.hcibooks.com.**
As a **"THANK YOU"** you will receive a **VALUABLE INSTANT COUPON** towards future book purchases
as well as a **SPECIAL GIFT** available only online! Or, you may mail this card back to us.

(PLEASE PRINT IN ALL CAPS)

First Name _____ MI. _____ Last Name _____

Address _____ City _____

State _____ Zip _____ Email _____

**1. Gender**
☐ Female ☐ Male

**2. Age**
☐ 8 or younger
☐ 9-12 ☐ 13-16
☐ 17-20 ☐ 21-30
☐ 31+

**3. Did you receive this book as a gift?**
☐ Yes ☐ No

**4. Annual Household Income**
☐ under $25,000
☐ $25,000 - $34,999
☐ $35,000 - $49,999
☐ $50,000 - $74,999
☐ over $75,000

**5. What are the ages of the children living in your house?**
☐ 0 - 14 ☐ 15+

**6. Marital Status**
☐ Single
☐ Married
☐ Divorced
☐ Widowed

**7. How did you find out about the book?**
*(please choose one)*
☐ Recommendation
☐ Store Display
☐ Online
☐ Catalog/Mailing
☐ Interview/Review

**8. Where do you usually buy reading about the books?**
*(please choose one)*
☐ Bookstore
☐ Online
☐ Book Club/Mail Order
☐ Price Club (Sam's Club, Costco's, etc.)
☐ Retail Store (Target, Wal-Mart, etc.)

**9. What attracts you most to a book?**
*(please choose one)*
☐ Title
☐ Cover Design
☐ Author
☐ Content

**10. What subject do you enjoy reading about the most?**
*(please choose one)*
☐ Parenting/Family
☐ Relationships
☐ Recovery/Addictions
☐ Health/Nutrition
☐ Christianity
☐ Spirituality/Inspiration
☐ Business Self-help
☐ Women's Issues
☐ Sports
☐ Pets

UHFG

TAPE IN MIDDLE; DO NOT STAPLE

# BUSINESS REPLY MAIL
FIRST-CLASS MAIL  PERMIT NO 45  DEERFIELD BEACH, FL

POSTAGE WILL BE PAID BY ADDRESSEE

Health Communications, Inc.
The Ultimate Series
3201 SW 15th Street
Deerfield Beach FL 33442-9875

FOLD HERE

The ULTIMATE Series

**Comments**

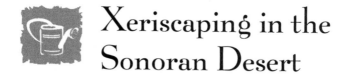

# Xeriscaping in the Sonoran Desert

*By Felice Prager*

To some, a garden must be lush and green with flowers and plants, a manicured lawn, bushes, hedges, and trees. We had one of those when we lived in New Jersey. Our summer chores were focused on mowing, raking, trimming, cutting back, removing weeds, and maintaining various projects we started. It was a labor of love, and it looked beautiful.

When we moved to Arizona's Sonoran Desert, however, we were aware that maintaining a garden would be nearly impossible. How could we get color in a backyard when water was a commodity and daily temperatures would burn most plants? When we built our house, the landscapers we hired tried to re-create New Jersey in our backyard, and we tried to maintain it. We had a lawn that we mowed when it was 110 degrees in the shade. We filled in patches with seed where the sun burned through what had been there. We planted things only to realize that if something isn't indigenous to the area, it will be difficult to keep it alive. We had a drip system to keep our bushes and plants healthy, but one by one, each item planted died. We thought our neighbors had more luck than we did with their yards, until we saw them putting in new plants that were just like the old ones.

Then we had a revelation. The revelation was fifteen years in the making, but we decided since we saw beauty in the desert, we should try to focus on that instead of trying to re-create what we used to know. With the teal blue sky adorned by wisps of clouds as a backdrop and burnished mountains sweeping the horizon, we decided to create a picture-postcard paradise in the desert right in our own backyard.

The concept is called xeriscaping. According to the State of Arizona Department of Water Resources, xeriscaping can take on many different looks depending on the gardener's taste. The idea is to decrease the harsh effects of the desert climate and increase energy efficiency by understanding the challenges and options available. We opted for the most minimalist approach. We wanted our yard to look natural, like the desert it used to be before man decided to cut it into developments. We wanted people to see our yard as a continuation of the desert arroyos adjacent to it.

We started by removing the lawn. It was not environmentally correct by any stretch of the imagination to use so much water. In its place, we decorated with sand, stones, and boulders. We transplanted cacti that had outgrown pots and put them into the ground. We did a great deal of research and learned which plants required full (intense) sunlight and which required shade or diffused sunlight. I opted for plants that needed little or no watering. The concept was that if it needed more than a bucket a month, it didn't fit into the plan. In fact, after planting the cacti, I became very aware of rain or lack of rain. I watered each plant (in the hot summer months) on the first of the month—unless it had rained.

What I noticed over time was that I didn't have to water anything if it belonged in the desert. Nature would provide. Overwatering tended to rot out the roots. To my surprise, everything produced by nature gave back presents. Cacti that just grew a little in pots grew huge in the ground. Some even flowered when they hadn't when they lived in pots. What started as rocks and some little plants is now a cactus garden of enviable proportion.

Many cacti also have another positive trait. If a cactus becomes overgrown, you can carefully remove a piece of it and plant it elsewhere. These cuttings grow into brand-new plants. In fact, if someone is visiting and comments on my cactus garden, I say, "Which is your favorite?" and I send them home with a cutting from it.

Like most Arizonans, we also have a swimming pool, which most of us who live in the desert find a necessity when it's 115 degrees outside. Having xeriscaping helps me feel less guilty about the water a pool uses.

My favorite of all my plants is my cereus in the front of my house. When we planted it about twenty years ago, it was about eighteen inches high and only had one stalk. I have a photo somewhere of my sons standing next to it on the first day of school, both pretty miserable because vacation is over. In the photo, both boys are taller than the plant was at the time. Today, the plant is taller than my house and has about twenty arms. I watch this plant more than all the others. It often gets scattered buds on the various arms. As these become larger, they bloom. The last time the cereus flowered, we had sixty-one flowers—yes, I counted—with a few opening every night. It takes about ten days from start to finish for one bud to become a flower. The flower opens slowly at sunset to a five-inch white flower. I've read that bats like them, but I haven't gone out to see them because I Don't Do Bats. In the morning, bees are drinking their last taste of nectar, and by about 8:00 AM when the sun is on them, they have completed their life cycle. Then they wither and die.

This morning, I went out to get the newspaper and there was one flower open. As I stood and admired it, a new neighbor walked by with her dog. She asked me what type of plant it was and I told her. She told me that she planned to re-landscape her property with a more natural look than the previous owners had. I just went to her house and handed her a small cutting from this plant. I told her the plant's history, and together, we planted it in her front yard. When she asked me what she had to do to keep it alive, I told her the truth: "Leave it alone. Admire it. Appreciate the beauty of the desert."

# My First Garden

*By Juliana Harris*

ave money . . . Gain peace of mind . . . Grow a garden . . . Call me and I'll start one for you with my wondrous machine."

This ad in our local newspaper last April was just the nudge I needed to plant my very first garden. I called and spoke with a Mr. Case ("Red Case, as in a case of beer") and, a few days later, he pulled up in a dazzling white pickup truck with his "wondrous machine" sitting in the back under an immaculate white cover.

I led him to the spot in my yard that gets the most sun and has good drainage. He nodded his approval at my choice of locale and went right to work, fastidiously uncovering the rototiller and proceeding to till the ten-by-fifteen-foot plot eight bone-jarring times.

When he finished, he announced, "You don't have a yard here, you have a rock quarry!" I asked his advice about fertilizing, and he told me since the land hadn't been used for a garden before, I really had to do very little to the soil. "Maybe a bag or two of cow manure and a little bit of lime and you'll be fine."

I chose the *New York Times Book of Vegetable Gardening* as my guide and went to the seed store, where I bought packets of marigold, lettuce, cucumber, zucchini, beet, bush bean, dill, and basil. I also bought a ten-pound bag of cow manure, but I couldn't find any bags of lime, so I decided to do without. Even though Mr. Case had done an excellent job of plowing, I found there were plenty of rocks left as I raked in the manure and began the fun of making neat rows for planting.

Every morning I rushed out to my garden to take a look at things. After two weeks I found a bright green trail of tiny leaves in my lettuce row. At that moment I felt exactly as I had when my babies first stirred inside my womb. Something I had planted was actually alive and growing!

By the time I left for a vacation in early July, the tomatoes were bearing green fruit, the zucchini were showing their first orange blossoms, the beets were three inches high, and I had harvested the last of the lettuce crop.

On the negative side, there was no sign of bush beans or basil, the marigolds were two feet high without a single bud on them (I decided they must be neuters), and the dill was straggly, to say the least. Strangely enough, the cucumbers had suddenly sprouted in late June, after I had completely given up hope on them.

As soon as I got back, I jumped out of the car and made a bee-line for my little plot. I let out a whoop of joy when I spotted the first buds on the marigolds. The blossoms on the zucchini had yielded three perfect emerald-green squash. The tomatoes were bigger, if not redder; the beets had grown another inch; and the cucumbers were really going gangbusters.

A few days after my return, my friend Carol stopped by for a chat. Maternal pride forced me to drag her to my garden to ooh and aah over my progeny.

"Just look at those cucumbers," I beamed fatuously, to which Carol replied, "Those aren't cucumbers."

"What do you mean those aren't cucumbers? They're growing in the cucumber row. Of course they're cucumbers!"

"I tell you, those aren't cucumbers. Cucumbers have hairy stems and grow along the ground. They do not grow straight up the way these plants do."

"Well then, these are a new breed of cucumber, a hybrid perhaps."

"You don't suppose they're weeds, do you?" Carol pondered.

"Impossible," I retorted. "Weeds don't grow in a nice straight line, neatly spaced the way these plants are doing."

But as soon as she left, I rushed to my handy reference book and frantically looked up the section on cucumbers, only to have my heart sink at the curious lack of resemblance between the illustration and what was growing in my cucumber row.

However, I refused to give up on my cucumbers until the dark day when I was doing some weeding around the foundation of the house and spied one of my "cucumber" plants nestling among the quack grass. I had been duped by a clever usurper from the weed world that had been masquerading as a cucumber while enjoying my devoted watering and tender ministrations!

My first impulse was to yank up every single one of those sneaks by their devious roots, but reason prevailed. I dubbed them the "Paraguayan Brag Plant" and glowed every time someone told me how nicely they were growing.

Oddly enough, when the Japanese beetle invasion began the following week, I was glad I had spared the weeds, because the iridescent kamikazes just loved to nibble on the "Brag Plant" while sparing my zucchini in the next row.

Now, as I write this, April is looming on my calendar once again. I look out my kitchen window at that bare plot of earth and can't wait to get started again. These are the lessons I'll remember this year:

- It pays to fertilize.
- Soil should be tested before planting.
- Soil imbalances should be corrected.
- Seeds should be started indoors.
- Cucumbers have hairy stems and grow along the ground.

# The Garden Saved My Life

By *Barbara Blossom Ashmun*

I still don't know who started the fire that changed my life on a Sunday night in July. I was away that weekend and drove home Monday morning past ranch houses with tidy front lawns. When I pulled into the driveway, I saw bright yellow crime scene tape strung across the porch. Black streaks smudged the eaves of the small green house I'd moved into only four months earlier. The blue spruce tree facing the kitchen was scorched brown, and jagged glass shards littered the front sidewalk. I picked my way around broken glass to the door where a notice read, "Do not enter. Conditions inside hazardous."

Woozy, I sank to my knees on the lawn. The ground was solid beneath me, and I ran my hands through cool blades of grass. *Please let me be dreaming*, I thought, *this must be a nightmare*. I pinched myself hard, but nothing changed. Across the street the same Photinia hedge framed my neighbor's gray bungalow.

I stood up, my body heavy and numb. Like a sleepwalker, I drifted toward my next-door neighbor's tan house and saw Anna rushing to meet me. She spoke with a thick Hungarian accent, her forehead corrugated with worry.

"Barbara, I'm so very sorry. Your house went on fire last night. No one knew where you were. Come inside, sit down here at the table," she urged.

I followed her woodenly into her immaculate house. Anna bustled around, pouring us freshly perked coffee and slicing homemade marble cake.

"Around eleven last night we heard this big boom and ran outside. Your house was on fire, flames was shooting out the roof. Steve from across the street was banging on your door to see if you was inside," she said.

"How did it start? What happened?" I asked, surprised I could still sip coffee from a china cup covered with tiny roses, like a normal person.

"The firemen said it was arson. They found kerosene in the garage. They want you should call this number right away." Anna handed me a business card.

I wanted to howl and weep, but instead I picked up the phone and called the fire station. Soon the doorbell rang, and a husky fireman walked me over to my house.

"I'll be right outside if you need me," he said. When I opened the front door an acrid stench filled my nostrils. Black soot covered the living room carpet. The jade plant was black and limp; the begonias had turned to tissue paper. The kitchen phone was a blue plastic puddle, and ivory laminate curled off the fronts of the cabinets. Flies buzzed in the dusty air.

I went to the bedroom, straight to the brass jewelry chest, and lifted the heavy lid, holding my breath. The diamond ring my Aunt Libby had left me still sparkled. I pushed it over my knuckle and rubbed my thumb across its hard surface, wishing she were still alive. *Give me strength; let me endure this,* I prayed silently.

Next I checked my home office, hoping the metal boxes holding ten years of garden slides were intact. I taught garden classes and lectured at garden shows; these slides were my living. I took one box outside into the sunlight and blew soot off the top. Inside, the slides were clean! I took a deep breath of relief and moved all the boxes into my car.

Waiting in the driveway, the fireman sent me a sympathetic look.

"An investigation will begin soon to track down the arsonist. But frankly, most of these crimes go unsolved. Take care," he said, patting me on the shoulder.

"Thanks," I blurted, swallowing tears, and fled to the yard. Before me pink summer phlox, golden yarrow, and purple bell-flowers bloomed steadily in the island beds like an alpine meadow. Since I'd moved to this sunny acre, I'd worked hard replanting peonies, penstemons, viburnums, and roses from my crowded city garden. They were already spreading their roots in the soil. I never dreamed my efforts to create a beautiful flower garden would begin on such rough ground. *Should I rebuild this house, or let it go and move again? Would I ever sleep soundly in this place? Who set this fire? Was it personal or random arson?* Questions buzzed through my mind like yellow jackets.

But love for the plants kept me going, as well as a furious determination not to give up. I grabbed a shovel and dug into the earth. Each angry stab made me stronger. I turned the soil over, then raked it smooth, daydreaming about what to plant. Roses and lavender will bloom here next summer, I vowed. I would not let this fire wreck my life. I would not uproot the garden and start all over again. I would stay for the plants; I would remain steady for the garden.

Despite my resolve, weeks of endless work wore me down—filing insurance claims; listing what was lost; cleaning, repairing, and storing what remained; buying essential clothing. Slogging through it all, step-by-step, I felt old and weary. I rented a small apartment two blocks from the house, close enough to walk to my garden.

Each morning I looked out my second-story apartment window into the sturdy branches of a big old oak tree. I pictured the tree standing stoically through wind, ice, rain, drought, and heat. The thick limbs looked powerful and immortal. I drew power from the oak's presence, receiving a daily transfusion of courage.

Every afternoon I walked to my garden to touch what I loved—lacy ferns, fragrant rosemary, and woolly lamb's ears that return every year, regardless of life's roller coaster. Indigo hydrangeas and pink peonies had bloomed in my old city garden, and now, transplanted, they carried on. The fire took my clothing, letters, and photographs, but I still had the garden to love and tend.

When 'Casa Blanca' lilies and Bourbon roses blew sweet perfume into the garden, I once again felt happy to be alive, even in the midst of chaos. Watering zinnias, digging out dandelions, and snapping off faded daylilies gave me purpose. As I swung the mattock into hard clay, tears flowed for my lost home and possessions. And yet joy bubbled up just as freely when I planted cranesbills and coral bells. A surprise visit from a friend bearing gifts from his garden lifted me up. Brown eggs from his chickens and homemade strawberry jam reminded me that life goes on.

I interviewed several contractors before finding one I trusted with such a daunting project. Most of them stood in the driveway holding clipboards, coldly professional, and I felt so alone. But Hal Slater sat with me under the flowering plum tree and regarded me with kind eyes. He quickly understood my love for the garden.

"Let's put huge windows in your office and bedroom, looking out on the garden. Let's bring light into dark places," he said. He showed me the silver lining, an improved home to replace the forty-year-old house.

But the insurance company dragged its heels and delayed approval for remodeling. Sheets of late summer rain poured through the burned roof, warping the oak floors. I visited the insurance adjustor, pleading for action.

"You're still a suspect in this fire. Until we clear you, we can't proceed," he said.

"Why would I set fire to my house when I'd just remodeled the kitchen?" I protested.

Heavy with defeat, I trudged to the car. Maybe I should just give up and abandon the whole mess. But then I remembered that my friend Betty's husband, Tony, was an attorney. I made an appointment to see him.

"I'll take care of this with one letter, don't you worry," he said, grinning. Two days later, the adjustor authorized Slater to start construction. Life looked good again.

While Slater remodeled, I threw myself into the garden. Old Concord grapevines leaning on sagging stakes begged for a sturdier home. I designed a tall rectangular arbor and hired a carpenter to build it.

In September, Michaelmas daisies opened hundreds of pink and blue flowers. I planted daffodils, tulips, and lily bulbs with a hopeful heart. By November I raked scarlet leaves into huge piles, flinging armloads of them into the wheelbarrow to take to the compost pile. I sang out loud to the staccato beat of the crew nailing shingles onto the roof. Soon the house would be ready to live in again.

I stayed on for the sake of the garden, but it was actually the garden that restored me to life. During my life's darkest passage, the garden healed me like a magic elixir. Twenty years later, fig trees bear honey-flavored fruit and burgundy grapes dangle from the grape arbor. Red and yellow dahlias flaunt voluptuous flowers beside coral and pink roses. I still rake leaves each fall and turn them into compost, thrilled to be tending the same garden for so many years.

# Hearts and Flowers

*By Melanie L. McCree*

Sleeping Beauty dreamed behind an impassible hedge of roses, fearsome with steely thorns and riotous with lush claret blooms. Fairy magic and heirloom grandifloras guarded the gates to a place apart. "Away defilers!" those roses warned. "Away despoilers, mockers, cheaters, thieves!" It is winter for her, but not for us. Never for us.

The fairy tales I read as a child ruined me. The world into which I had been born was excruciatingly mundane—no quests, no treasure, no magic at all. I couldn't stand it. Faced with the ordinary—math class, for example—I would race to the door in my imagination and dive through. In fairyland, I could mount a bay gelding, bow over my shoulder, blossoms woven into my long, thick braid, free as the North Wind and merry as a pocketful of gold. The Black Castle of Pre-Algebra would be far away—until the bell rang, and then horse and bow and freedom (and braid) would all vanish, and there I would be, in a plastic chair with a half desk bolted to one side, wondering whether I would actually need all that stuff on the chalkboard, currently being erased.

I couldn't help it . . . didn't want to. Unthinkable, to trade magic for math.

In any fairy story, the hero must face the Wild, a place of thicket and meadow, bramble and blossom older than time, bigger than space. Impossible roses are born in this Wild. The gates to every secret path start in it, and every labyrinth winds through it. The journey is always difficult and generally results in permanent damage—and if the hero is lucky, he gets a happy ending. If he's not, he gets real life.

I got older and went out into the world and lived here and there, in apartments I could afford, gray places with old bark dust and rangy juniper and token scrub pines huddling like bad-tempered hermits. I couldn't root anywhere. I wasn't getting enough sun. A story makes its own place, but you need a plot of land to grow flowers.

Then I found, for a reasonable amount, a duplex on a big lot. The yard was a misery, buried under fat-bladed grass, morning glories squeezing everything until it suffocated. But there were roses there, poor orphans, brittle-boned and skeletal, quietly giving up hope by the driveway. Roses in distress. I had an earnest discussion with the landlords. Glassy-eyed, I put my money down.

I waited six months before moving the bushes, because I wanted to do it right. I bought fertilizer, peat moss, sand, compost, shovels, gloves, shears. I watched DVDs. I brought home stacks of books. There were two varieties on the property, from what I could tell, suffering together in little self-defensive clumps, and I would space them properly, in two rows that curved along the driveway in a graceful half circle.

I thought about my half circle of rosebushes constantly. I talked about roses until my family ran from the room. Then I talked to my coworkers. Then I talked to strangers. Finally, on a gray, cold day at the end of winter, I went out into the yard, placed the shovel, and stepped on it.

The blade passed easily through the first half foot of soil and rammed into something with a shudder and a dull clank. Rock, I thought, and pulled the shovel loose and replaced it, meaning to dig around. Again, the impact and the shudder and the clank. Then again, and again. This was not just one rock. This was a layer of rocks, with the purest clay I'd ever seen underneath, orange and chunky and apparently serving as a foundation for the entire property. I leaned on the shovel and took comfort in explicit language.

In front of me was a sorry excuse for a rosebush. It hadn't bloomed the year before, it hadn't even really bothered with leaves, and I had no idea what color the flowers were supposed to be. Five thin stalks with ragged tips, exhausted and sickly, were poking up out of what had to be the worst soil in the entire world. I sighed deeply and stomped some more on the shovel.

It took me fifteen minutes, but I dug my first hole. Slimy with clay and sweat, more evil-tempered by the second, I dug that hole, and found not one rose, but two, planted perhaps five inches apart. No wonder the bush hadn't bloomed. Who would do a thing like this? I set them on the ground, poor little root-balls, three stalks on one, two on the other. I was going to need help.

I enlisted my nephew, a big guy, twenty years old and determined. We dug two new holes wide and deep to allow plenty of room for roots to grow and added absurd amounts of sand and compost to the clay, then settled the transplants. I grinned at my nephew, delighted. We had a routine established—we'd be done in no time.

We dug another rose free. It took a while. We punched the earth, dripping and cursing, until we could carefully jiggle our prize from the ground. It was two roses, buried together.

Almost every rose in the yard had been buried two and even three plants together. In one case, four emaciated limbs above an enormous bud union turned out to be four roses, packed so tightly in their rock-walled prison that they had absorbed each other like white cells engulfing a virus. Their single, lunatic root was hopelessly misshapen. I could do nothing for them, and I didn't try; I was glad for an extra hole. The total number of roses kept rising. Ten were expected. Nineteen showed up. I needed a chiropractor.

When I wasn't digging, I was arguing with myself, standing by my living room window gazing down at thick February mud and shriveled bushes with stalks like chin hairs. I knew I was obsessed. Normal people didn't put time and money into flowers that weren't theirs, that might not even live. I couldn't justify what I was doing. I had passed through the door again, and imagination had swallowed me. And then one day, there were no more roses to move, and everything was brown and gray; all that was left to me was worry.

The time passed. The days got longer and the nights warmer, and rain covered the world like a shroud. I stared out the window and called myself all kinds of names. I was ashamed of my preoccupation, of the money wasted and the energy burned on something of no worth, something anyone else would have left to die. Unsavory as the truth was, it was still the truth, that there was no Wild, not on Earth, but there were always bills and taxes and chores. Endless, unstoppable responsibility. I would sometimes cry, my forehead on the glass, until the cold could soothe my head.

Then, one morning, I saw leaves.

Not many. The roses in yards all over town were already glorious, and my poor orphans, in comparison, were consumptive. But this was new growth, healthy and green, and I went out to my plants and stood above them and beamed, and spoke to them lovingly, and was late to work. There was no excuse I could give, and I didn't try to find one. My roses deserved better. That night I stood at the window and watched the sun turn straw into gold.

Do not apologize for loving. Spring opens the heart, and the heart cannot be closed again. This is what hurts about love, and this is why it never matters that love might hurt.

As I write this, my roses are blooming: pink, and red, and over by the garage, yellow. The floribunda bushes are rangy, but they are covered in blooms like butterflies, and they will fill in better next year. The tallest pink rose is higher than my head, and its fragrance is a perfect kiss. The deepest red blooms are on a bush with only three thin stalks. The leaves around it are edged in olive and trimmed in gold, and the flowers are wine velvet and would grace any table in the Castle of the Beast.

I talk to them all the time, because I love them. I am hopeless with it. They will need plenty of care to be what they are supposed to be, and they will get it. Trowel in hand, dirt and sweat smeared over me—soles to crown—wearing a distant gaze and ignoring the scratches on my hands, I am dreaming, eyes wide open. I can't help myself, and I don't want to.

My roses are growing, heavy with blooms, wicked with thorns. Tall as a tale, real as magic. Guarding a place where winter never comes.

# Think Circles

*By Veronica Cullinan Lake*

found the house I wanted. It rested on one hundred feet of property. The house occupied only fifty feet. The rest was filled with trees, bushes, vines, and flowering plants all smashed together into a jungle. Two seasonal plants next to the front door would have been enough for me.

At age eighty-two, the owner was planning to move to a retirement home. When we met she asked what my plans for the house were, if I bought it. "To keep it just the way it is—small, with its own charm," I replied. She told me that her father built it with his own hands.

"What about the garden?" she asked, turning her face slowly toward it.

"As a city girl, I know little about gardens," I replied honestly, "but I'll do my best."

"When I sell, I'll sell it you," she promised. From time to time I would leave notes in her mailbox. Two years later her daughter called. "We're selling the house as is. It's either you or a contractor who's going to rebuild. My mother is sure you won't destroy her garden."

By the time I bought the house, it needed serious repairs. The contractor I hired, not able to drive his trucks up the driveway, yelled, "Cut some of these branches, get those fir trees off the windows, clean all that brush away from the walls. I need access to the house." So I hired a man on a bicycle who cruised the neighborhood looking for work. He sawed away and ripped up any obstructions.

When spring came I couldn't make my way into the house. Daffodils sprouted up willy-nilly in the driveway. Wisteria and honeysuckle choked the trees. Vines and giant irises stopped the lawn mower. I needed a machete.

Instead I called in a landscaper. "It's a jungle in there," he said. "It'll take three or four days to cut it all down. I charge eight hundred dollars a day. Later you can put in a nice pool with concrete around it." That wasn't what I wanted. I called another landscaper. He drove up in a Cadillac with classical music blaring and sighed when he got out of the car. "This is a mess. There is nothing I can do for you," he stated firmly. "It's too big of a job and I'm short of men."

I pleaded, "Could you just clear it out a little?"

"All I can give now is advice," he said. "Think in circles. Stand in one place, look at the leaves. If you find five plants with the same leaf, dig up three. Keep going until you have some empty space."

I walked to the hardware store and bought a shovel, clippers, and a branch trimmer.

I spent two entire summers thinking circles. Passersby comments ranged from, "Never knew there was a house behind all that," to "That's a lot of work for one woman, especially one your age," to an encouraging "Looking good!"

By the third summer, I had fallen in love with the lilacs, rose of Sharon, tulips, tiger lilies, and giant irises. I could mow some of the grass. There was even a small crooked path leading to the house. While tripping over the remaining vines, I identified forsythias, hydrangea, rhododendron, and azaleas. They would stay, but what about the rest—the unknown?

Looking out the train window going back to Manhattan, I spotted the same bushes laying along the railroad tracks. It dawned on me. The unidentifiable were weeds. Wild things were growing happily in my garden. So I hired a man to dig up anything that matched what I had seen near the tracks.

Friends visiting from New York remarked, "You know, your entire property is a garden from the street up to your door. You need to clear out a space. Get rid of everything within ten feet of your house. This is scary! Perverts could be hiding behind those bushes. Get a dog that kills on command. In fact, get two of them." I cleared the space, but passed on the dogs.

By spring I had room enough to walk around the bushes, so I decided to cut everything into a ball and look at their leaves again. Twelve bushes kept branching out.

A landscaper identified them as crab apple trees. These, plus the rose of Sharon bushes (all thirty of them), were marching into the cleared space. A gardener dug up all but three of the crab apple trees, a giant fruit tree throwing pears onto my neighbor's deck, and about ten of the pink, purple, and white rose of Sharon. After four summers I finally had a garden!

With a big smile on my face, I put a cushion on the wicker chairs on the porch and invited the original owner to tea on her eighty-eighth birthday. Seeing the smile on her face, I knew we were both deeply happy we had kept our promises to each other.

# My Ultimate Garden Project

*By Lisa Scott*

We were lucky enough to move into a big three-quarter-acre city lot with just one little garden bed. That meant we got to transform the yard ourselves: a gardener's dream—the ultimate chance to get our hands dirty. Each year we've taken on a major backyard project: rototilling deep flower beds, installing a pergola and patio, fencing off the yard, adding an arbor, tucking in a playhouse and swing set. But my dream project was a water garden. Maybe it was the memory of the beautiful waterfalls from our Hawaiian honeymoon, or the fact that I've had fish since I was five. But I wouldn't be happy until I had an oasis in my backyard. And my husband promised me one—if we took down our above-ground pool.

That was a tough sell. I love swimming. Admittedly, the pool was cold and hard to keep clean. And in upstate New York, we really only get three months' use out of it each year. But as a woman who spent 75 percent of her childhood summers in the pool, it took me two years to decide to part with it. But finally, I was ready to take on my ultimate garden project.

I wanted to make a big splash. A local water garden coach told me 40 percent of his customers are people coming back to make their pond bigger. And bigger ponds are easier to keep balanced and clean. So yes, a big splash was a must—without the big bucks. But the plans I had in mind could add up to a five-figure price tag if we hired someone to do it. So this was going to be a definite do-it-yourselfer.

Good thing I didn't realize how much do-it-yourselfing I would be doing.

The work started long before the shovel hit the dirt. The year before we broke ground, I began collecting rocks from our yard waste dump. The guys who work there called me when people dropped off rocks. I made dozens of trips, piling them into my SUV, banging fingers and stubbing my toes. I even braved a thunderstorm when someone left loads of huge flat stones and beautiful old pavers. (I took a break when it started to hail.) It was a landscaper's jackpot.

I needed even more rocks, though. I found someone who was dismantling a rock wall, and he let me raid his backyard. I even joined our local geological society to collect beautiful accent pieces at local quarries. In the end, I gathered more than a thousand dollars' worth of free rocks.

I spent all winter reading garden books and dreaming about my perfect pond. When spring rolled around, I took a "Build Your Own Water Garden" class. They admitted I had an ambitious project: a twenty-two–by–twenty-two–by-two-foot with two waterfalls and a small river winding around the back. My husband would add a lower level to our deck to come over the edge of the pond, while I worked on the pond itself.

I bought the biggest kit they had and started removing the pool, adjoining deck section, and shrubs. That took a month's worth of work on the weekends. (I contracted poison ivy on my face and hands at this point.) There was sand under the pool to dispose of (we dumped that under our deck) and several yards of decorative stones to remove from around the pool. (Those went around our playhouse.) And then there was the pool deck to dispose of. It was frustrating work with little reward: I had no evidence of my dream pond yet.

But finally, it was time to start the pond. The garden coach advised me to dig it by hand, because an excavator couldn't be finessed to create the plant shelves. But after several weekends of digging in the rain around big rocks and roots (and crying at night, wondering if the project would ever get done), my brother offered to rent an excavator and dig it for me. Cool. I decided to start working on the waterfall.

Not so cool. My hands started going numb at night from hauling 150 concrete blocks to build the base of the falls and river. And did I mention the excavator broke when we rented it, and there was no one at the store to fix it? My brother and husband tinkered with it while I fretted that the project really never would get done. But they repaired it and finally dug out the pond.

I was left with mounds of excavated dirt to landscape around the pond. (I became one with the wheelbarrow, which left brand-new calluses on my hands.) And just like the garden coach said, the excavator left a shelfless hole in the ground, so I had to climb in and create shelves with dirt and concrete blocks. My young children asked me daily why the pond wasn't done yet. Three months into the project, I was wondering the same thing.

Meanwhile, the free rocks weren't my only money-saving scheme. I dug up lily pads from my brother's pond that sat in buckets in my driveway. I brought home a few yards of free mulch from the yard waste dump. That sat on my patio for months. I shopped sales for plants and swapped with friends.

Soon I was ready for a big step: burying the hose and the filter box. Not quite remembering all the details from the class four months earlier, I drilled a hole in the wrong spot in the filter box and had to repair it. Then I wasn't sure exactly where to place it. I dug up and reburied it three times (and later decided it should have been even deeper). I had the garden center on speed dial, and I'm sure they were getting ready to start blocking my frequent calls.

My husband's work on the deck progressed, but he did take a break to finally help me lay down the huge thirty-by-thirty-foot section of liner. Then we had to spread four yards of pebbles over that and add boulders. All those rocks I had collected had to be designed into two waterfalls and a river. (I still didn't have enough. I had to dismantle one of my own rock walls!) My seven-year-old son lost interest in the whole thing when he learned I wasn't building the river as a playground for his trucks and army men.

I was at the height of the project, going to bed exhausted after working from sunrise to sunset. I started to panic. There was a huge hole in my backyard. It seemed so giant, much bigger than I'd planned, and it was taking so long! Was I in over my head?

But finally, we were ready to add the water. It was so dirty, we pumped it out and started over. It was still cloudy, and I was worried it would never be clear. But in a few days, we could see to the bottom and spot the few "tester" fish we'd tossed in. My five-year-old daughter showed up with her snorkel gear, and when I told her she wouldn't be swimming with the fishes, she was suddenly crying for the old pool. Had I made a mistake embarking on my ultimate gardening project?

I had more landscaping to do, but I was sidelined for two weeks after spraining my hand lifting rocks. (I welcomed the break.) Next, I mulched the landscaping as my husband finished the deck, and we finally laid down those pavers to create a small patio. Our job was complete a mere six months after we started it. It was just as beautiful as I had dreamed it would be.

The first few days, I'd gaze at it, wondering if it really was there, if I'd really done that all by myself, if I was dreaming. We celebrated with an open house to show it off to our neighbors who'd been peeking in on our work all summer long.

We spent more money than we expected (about the cost of a really, really nice family vacation even with all of my cost-cutting measures). But I feel like I'm on vacation every day when I sit on the deck and watch our twenty-five koi fish gliding through the crystal clear water. It's instant therapy; the honest-to-God best addition to my life since having my kids. And my enjoyment is tenfold knowing we did it ourselves.

Of course, I'm not really done. You never are. I'll probably be forever tinkering with the waterfalls and plantings. (Moving just one rock changes the way the water flows and sounds. And you can lose a few hours doing that, because once you move one, you're sure to move another.)

I'm sure I'll come up with something new to do in our yard. I am a gardener, after all, and I won't be happy unless I have a project in the works to keep my hands dirty.

# Through the Seasons

# Shades of Summer

*By Lola Di Giulio De Maci*

We all lived on the same block—my grandma and grandpa, my Aunt Mary and Uncle Pete, my cousins Frank, Virginia, and Dick, and all my friends—and we all shared a vegetable garden. It wasn't just an ordinary garden; it was a garden that belonged to all of us.

Our garden grew right in the center of a whole city block, and our houses made a perfect border for its bounty. Our front doors faced four different streets with four different street names, and our back doors opened to this colorful collage of vine-ripened tomatoes, bell peppers, zucchini, string beans, carrots, and sweet corn. Clusters of lilies of the valley, bright blue morning glories, and tall sun-yellow sunflowers roamed wildly in and out of the vegetable plants, unable to be tamed.

But I think the best part of sharing these vegetables and flowers with our neighbors was the many paths that led from one back door to another. After meandering through narrow dirt paths, my back-yard found my friends' backyards, where we would spend hours coloring, making clothes for our paper dolls, and eating the grapes we picked from the many arbors that shaded front and back porches.

And Grandma's house, which was right across the driveway from Aunt Mary's, could be reached a lot quicker by way of this pastoral route than by walking the sidewalks that outlined the front yards. Her screen door was always open, and she was always cooking. As I approached her backyard, I could smell the hot, fresh tomatoes from the garden being canned in the basement, the boiling water racing rapidly around sterilized Mason jars. And I knew instantly that we would have enough tomato sauce for Grandma's spaghetti and lasagna all winter long.

I would spend hours wandering through this garden, picking fresh tomatoes off the vine and eating them whole. On many warm summer days, that would be my entire lunch—just tomatoes and salt. I would sit in the shade of a cornstalk and let the juice of the tomato run freely down my arm. And then for dessert, I would disappear down the path into Aunt Mary's kitchen for her homemade pound cake, the same pound cake I make for my family today.

There were no fences or concrete walls separating neighbors from one another back then. No answering machines or online services keeping one human voice from another. Whenever you wanted to call someone and say, "Good morning, how are you?" there was always someone at the other end of the line to answer you.

I don't know if that magical garden exists today, but I do know I haven't seen anybody canning tomatoes in a Mason jar for a long, long time. But someday soon, just for old time's sake, I'm going to pick a ripe tomato off the vine, find the shade of a tall cornstalk, and let the juice of the tomato run freely down my arm.

# The Stars of Bethlehem

*By Annmarie B. Tait*

Yesterday, the sunny crisp April morning inspired me once again to search our front yard for the Stars of Bethlehem. On the short jaunt from the front door to the car, my eyes darted back and forth surveying the freshly sprouting lawn. Eventually on one of my early morning trots, I know I'll catch a glimpse of the delicate white blossom poking its head through the blades of grass, and I will smile. If spring arrived each year to the grandeur of an opening ceremony, I'm convinced my annual discovery of the first Star of Bethlehem flower would be it.

I've heard some people boldly call these blossoms weeds and declare them an eyesore. To me, they are God's gift to children who do not have open fields through which to rollick and discover the joy of wildflowers. The Stars of Bethlehem often grow between the cracks in the sidewalk, along with buttercups and violets. Many are the mothers who treasure the memory of tiny hands overflowing with the gift of fresh-picked wildflowers. My mother was no exception.

I grew up in the city with neatly numbered streets and backyards just as neatly divided by iron hairpin fences. My family tree is planted where there are no open fields trimmed in a rainbow of wildflowers. Even so, nature bursts forth undaunted by concrete and steel. Whether you live among the neatly numbered streets of the city or the wide-open spaces of the country, Mother Nature does not hide from the heart that seeks to discover her fascinating presence.

On a little patch of earth enclosed by a hairpin fence, my mom and dad grew the sweetest cantaloupe and juiciest tomatoes I have ever tasted. In our backyard, the violets and Stars of Bethlehem flourished along the hairpin fence that divided our yard from our neighbor's. It was there that I often gathered a bouquet for Mom. How vividly I remember running up onto the porch and through the back door, hardly able to contain my excitement. Mom always took the flowers from me with great fanfare, fussing over how precious they were. But more than that, Mom proved it, at least in my eyes, by treating those little flowers with the same respect she gave to long-stemmed roses. Without hesitation she trimmed the stems and placed them in fresh water, which she changed every day until the flowers wilted beyond revival.

My mom's birthday was in early spring, around the time the wildflowers are just beginning to bloom. When I was old enough to afford it, I always sent her fresh-cut flowers from the florist along with a note that read, "These are just to hold you over." She arranged them in small vases all over the house, cheering up every room with a tiny taste of spring. But I knew the message on the card brought her much more pleasure than the florist shop flowers ever could.

My birthday is only two weeks after my mom's. In this short span of time, the violets and Stars of Bethlehem reach their peak. So, when I went home on my birthday to enjoy my mom's cooking, I always made sure to have a handful of the Stars of Bethlehem with a sprinkling of violets and buttercups thrown in just for good measure.

Usually when I arrived, Dad would be sitting at the dining room table poring over his seed catalogs, while Mom waited in the kitchen with a jelly jar glass half filled with water. I'd give Dad a kiss and head straight for the kitchen, knowing she was waiting there for me. As I approached her, I'd draw the flowers out from behind my back and hand them to her accompanied by a wide smile and a kiss on the cheek. She'd smile back and hug the little girl in me that has never grown up. Into the jelly jar vase the flowers went to be trimmed and cared for each day as if they were long-stemmed roses. To her they were just as precious. How I cherish the memory of our little ritual now that she is gone.

No matter how old I was, my mom never seemed surprised that I kept this little tradition going. In her mind I was no age in particular. I was just a child—her child—with a fistful of the Stars of Bethlehem. When I came through that door, we were both young again, even if only for the moment our eyes met, as the flowers drifted slowly from my hands into hers.

# Summer Nights

*By Cookie Curci*

Long before I began nurturing my own backyard herb garden, I spent my summers watching my Nonna Isolina passionately cultivate her productive garden of carrots, zucchini, string beans, peppers, tomatoes, Swiss chard, rosemary, garlic, escarole, onions, parsley, and arugula in the Santa Clara Valley of California.

As a child, I sat for hours high in Nonna's backyard walnut tree observing her at work in her beloved garden; other times, I filled my shirttails with fruit picked from her orchard trees. I ate apricots, peaches, winesap apples, and purple boysenberries until my stomach ached.

On these occasions, I was unhappily introduced to Nonna's herb garden and the medicinal greens growing there, like chamomile, parsley, rosemary, lemongrass, spearmint, peppermint, witch hazel, and a bitterly pungent plant called arugula. Nonna employed these herbs regularly to treat my childhood bellyaches.

Nonna loved life as she loved her garden and believed there was something new to be learned about each day. I recall how the two of us would walk hand in hand among her prolific vegetable garden, observing her young bean sprouts bursting through the crusty earth; how she would point out the young seedlings that were destined to grow and the ones that would die. Speaking to me in her native Italian language, she would say, "That which does not grow dies." She applied this philosophy to her everyday life as well. Change and growth uplifts us and generates life. Just like Nonna's young seedlings, the grand essentials of life are nourishment, growth, and love.

At the break of dawn, Nonna could be found in her garden sipping on a cup of strong coffee while she surveyed the work that awaited her. She read the cloud formations each morning in order to predict impending shifts in the weather and precipitation. Low-flying, pillowlike cumulus clouds were her favorite, for they foretold of sunny, fair weather ahead. At night, long after the sun had set, she'd return to the garden to defend it from snails and other crusty crawlers, plucking them off one by one and tossing them into a bucket.

For Nonna, working in her garden was an everyday ritual. She'd done it so often, and for so long, as to almost become invisible at it. Nonna had always loved her garden, bringing to it every little scrap of knowledge and experience she gathered in the fields and orchards of her Old Country.

Growing up in a small coastal village in Italy, near the Adriatic Sea, she learned early on that fish was the best fertilizer for fruit trees, and cucumbers caught the best sunlight when planted near a northern fence, and the best time to plant parsley was on Good Friday. In March, on the Feast of St. Joseph, she seeded her flowering herbs, knowing instinctively just when to pick them and which ones to use for what illness: chamomile tea for a good night's sleep, rosemary and mint to soothe a stubborn cold, basil to relax a nervous stomach, and sage to calm everything from a headache to a sore throat.

Sweet basil hugged the stepping-stones along the garden path. Its pungent aroma filled our nostrils and lingered fragrantly on our clothing.

March was for Grandma, and for all of us who enjoyed her bountiful garden, a time of great anticipation, a time of waiting for the burst of vegetable blossoms that came as a prelude to the flowers that were to grace her garden beds.

In mid-August, a dazzling combination of annuals and perennials filled the sun-drenched plots of Nonna's glorious garden. She knew that bright blossoms stood up best against the harsh rays of the noonday sun; for that reason golden sunflowers, 'Silver Cup' Lavatera, hollyhocks, delphiniums, and snapdragons filled her sunniest locations. Nearby, in rutted rows, grew white pelargoniums, warm-hued 'Goldsturm,' and 'Indian Summer' rudbeckia.

Lavender, marjoram, rosemary, sage, savory, and thyme were planted in sun-drenched areas of the garden. Nurtured in raised beds along the walkway were herbs that favored full sun and rich, moist soil, such as basil, coriander, parsley, tarragon, and fennel.

I believe Nonna's ability to grow things was part instinct, part knowledge, and, I suspect, a bit of magic tossed in for good measure. In her garden, Nonna could slow down the quickly passing days and feel closer to life. It was her Old World belief that a garden brought prosperity and harmony to a home.

It was many years later that I paid my Nonna and her garden a final visit. As I walked up the pathway, I could smell the inviting aroma of her Italian tomato sauce bubbling on the stove like an eternal volcano. She was well into her eighties by then, but still an avid gardener and an excellent cook. Like a lot of things I remember from that day, the fragrance of her budding spring flowers mingled with the aroma of her simmering tomato sauce remains unchanged and forever in my memory.

It was a bright, sun-washed day, and I wasn't at all surprised to find Nonna puttering in her backyard herb garden. She was all alone now and her garden had grown steadily smaller through the years. But, as always, she continued to revere the growing of things and the procession of the seasons. Remarkably, she could still pinpoint the arrival of the summer solstice without glancing at a calendar.

The day of my visit, Nonna didn't readily notice my arrival. She was too busy weeding her seedlings and playing tug-of-war with the roots of a stubborn dandelion weed. Time had engraved Grandma's hands and face with a pattern of deeply set wrinkles. Her once-sparkling eyes were dimmer now and framed by a set of well-defined crow's feet. But still they reflected that same familiar twinkle of welcome. From beneath her sunbonnet, a stray wisp of white hair fluttered in the warm afternoon breeze.

I watched Grandma's small, timeworn hands move diligently among her garden plants. As she walked along her garden path, her old cat, Chulet, traced her footsteps, taking halfhearted swings at Nonna's dangling apron strings. I remembered when the aged cat was a frolicking young kitten determined to chase tantalizing butterflies and plump grasshoppers that thronged to the garden. Nonna was younger then, too. Her long white hair was a dark brunette in those days, showing only traces of gray, and the stubborn roots of a dandelion weed would have been no match for her strong, nimble fingers.

I spent that night at Nonna's, sleeping in the same cozy bedroom I'd known so well as a child, the same hand-stitched quilt tenderly comforting the foot of my bed. I could hear Nonna softly tracing her footsteps from room to room as she went about her nightly ritual, latching the windows and locking the doors. My room was her last stop on her nightly sojourn. She carefully latched my windows, tightly tucked in the corners of my bed, then, as she'd done a thousand times before, she leaned over and kissed me good night, and for a brief, wonderful moment I was nine years old again.

A warm night and a full moon inspired me to open my bedroom window overlooking Nonna's garden. As if expecting something remarkable to happen, I keenly surveyed Nonna's herbs and flowers under the moonlight.

I remembered how her herbal remedies were almost magical in their curative powers—perhaps I was hoping to see some of that magic. I don't know how long I sat staring out the window.

The last glimmer of moonlight was just about to fade behind a passing cloud when Nonna's stately sunflowers, stiff as fence posts just seconds before, suddenly began shimmying violently like hootchy-kootchy dancers. Silhouetted against the moon, the imposing row of sunflowers formed a long, rhythmic conga line in this uniquely choreographed dance. A moment later, rosemary, mint, and oregano stems, like scrawny ballerinas, began to pirouette and sway as they joined in the impromptu minuet.

Summer blossoms suddenly unfolded, filling the air with tantalizing fragrance.

A flock of night birds feasting on the sunflowers had caused them to buckle and sway in the herky-jerky motion. Tiny winged insects and hungry night crawlers dining on the succulent herbs had encouraged the rhythmic movement of the burgeoning blossoms. Nonna's garden had come to life, just for me, and its heart beat softly to the rhythm of summer winds and fluttering birds' wings.

The next day, Nonna insisted I take home some seedlings from her garden: a piece of this, a smidgen of that, and a handful of her finest sunflower seeds. She searched carefully through her garden for the perfect seedlings—uprooting several oregano, chamomile, and rosemary plants, including the bitter arugula.

That was my last visit with Nonna. Today, her chamomile, oregano, and arugula grow thickly along my garden fence. Although I've never had occasion to use Nonna's plants to treat a bellyache, I feel better just knowing they're out there. Her tall, golden sunflowers grace my garden like her sunny smile. And, as I grow older, I've come to appreciate all that Nonna taught me. I treasure her old stories and beliefs, and I'm grateful she left behind a small part of herself that grows in a garden of remembrances that lives on and on.

On hot summer nights, when I open my bedroom window overlooking my garden, a sigh of sage, lavender, and sweet basil rise to greet me like Nonna's gentle touch. Her herbs and flowers are a gift of love that binds us and promises to keep us together through the years.

Sometimes, on a rare, moonlit night, when a warm wind blows

and night birds invade my sunflowers, my garden comes to life just for me—and somehow I know that pleases Nonna.

Joseph Addison, in his wisdom, once wrote, "The grand essentials to happiness in this life are something to do, something to love, and something to hope for." Nonna found all of these in her beloved garden.

# Smiling Like Mona in the Garden

*By Janice A. Farringer*

When I first saw the little wooden town house painted faded pumpkin, all I wanted to do was see if I could move in right away. The street of almost identical duplexes nestled in the woods was my hope for some normality after being laid off, moving back to a town I love, and looking for an affordable place to rent. Life had been upside down for several months and I wanted to nest.

The inside was fine. The back deck looked out onto a nature preserve. The ample wooded side yard bordered a walking trail that sloped down to a creek. Everything out there was overgrown, strangled with weeds, and dotted with poison ivy. Whoever lived here before was no gardener.

I brought my friend Kris to see the place just to make sure I wasn't being starry-eyed, and she, being a great gardener, looked around the yard with a practiced eye. The rental agent worried that I would be put off by the jungle. She started telling us that perhaps she could do this and that about mowing and get someone over to cut some things back. Kris just smiled. She told the woman that I would know what to do. I grinned back. Gardeners smile like that among themselves. I was home.

The boxes inside were left for months. I had a reachable bed, couch, and kitchen, and I escaped outside. I cleared and pulled and dug and watched the sun. This was a shade garden. I saw it. It wasn't there yet, but I saw it. The trees were old and high. My other gardens had all been sunny. This would be new.

The first thing to go was the old gnarly butterfly bush. I cut it back and cut it back—and then it died. Ground gained. There was some boxwood along the drive and there were some azaleas. After I cleared a few weeds, I discovered they had been planted on a steep downslope, probably to stop erosion. With little level ground, I proceeded to make some. High flexible edging filled with store-bought dirt gave me a start on my first bed.

With every small infrastructure victory, I began the experiment that is gardening. My problem was that I knew more about plants that need sun than shade lovers. I planted familiar things and they failed. Hmm, *think shade, think shade. Think dry shade,* every gardener's nemesis. The tall pines and pecan trees sucked the ground dry on my hill, leaving pine straw and clay. I started a compost heap.

Over time, I made the transition. I went down to the woods in the spring and dug up native ferns. Gorgeous. They were moved maybe fifty yards, but it made all the difference. A friend contributed hellebores, and I planted the heirloom hydrangeas I rooted from my former garden. I planted Japanese forest grass in pots with chartreuse hostas and white begonias. Creeping Jenny crept around and settled into the crevices.

I moved daylilies I had carted back from another city up near the road to a tiny patch of sun and surrounded them with impatiens under the pink rose of Sharon. It took bags and bags of dirt to fill an enormous pot I got at a nursery's going-out-of-business sale. In it I grew sun lovers on my driveway where the sun baked them into bloom.

On the back deck, hostas plumed up out of pots draped with gold and green ivy. Lots of pots. I have a tree in a pot out there. I am surrounded by every shade of green, from lime to deep blue.

I don't try for perfect. Heavens, there is too much to be done to think of perfect. The forest might swoop down on all of this again, any minute. Swallow it whole. I like to think my garden in the woods looks like the leftovers of what might once have been here. Maybe the purple oxalis along the edge of the woods just blew in on the wind. Those asters are new but may look accidental one day, if I'm lucky.

This spring the rental agent called me at work. She said she needed to come over that afternoon. She needed to get in to measure and wanted to tell me that the house would be put up for sale. It took me a moment to breathe. My garden was nearly four years old.

Sometimes things happen for the best. I didn't take time to mope. I had to do something. If a house could be bought on short notice, I would do it.

In the middle of a year of bad economic news, I bought my garden—I mean, my house. Mortgaged, but mine. I dig. I trim and pull. I touch and talk and deadhead. I water sparingly and fertilize slowly. I smile like Mona in the mornings when I take my dog out. I have to see what changed overnight. See what will bloom today. See if the deer came through. My daily silent rounds of my piece of ground are sacred.

My garden is my excuse to talk with strangers at garden centers and ask questions of horticulturalists. I trek through botanical gardens, arboretums, and friends' gardens with an eye toward stealing their ideas. Picking viola colors in the fall is a major ritual to find just the right combination of colors to fit my mood this year. I fret over whether it will be purple with yellow faces or white and blue this year. Maybe I'll go solid yellow.

And the names, oh my. Lisianthus and Lespedeza. Calycanthus and Artemisia.

Agapanthus, Dianthus, Clematis, Hemerocallis, and spurge. Poetry in a seed catalog on a winter's night. The stuff of dreams for spring in the garden.

So I am home outside for most of the year. Good weather and bad dirt is what I have. But the compost is cooking, the birds are singing, and the deer will come for dinner at the most inopportune time. So come on over. I'll show you my garden.

# Montana Transplants

*By Cathy Slovensky*

*Earth is here so kind, that just tickle her with
a hoe and she laughs with a harvest.*

—Douglas William Jerrold

Several years ago, via a change in employment for my husband, Bill, our family was transplanted from the mountains of Montana to the wine valley of Walla Walla, Washington. My family has deep roots in Montana, so the thought of leaving family and friends behind was difficult, not to mention leaving a house and gardens that we had lovingly tended for nearly twenty years.

Not wanting to pull our son, Will, out of school in the middle of his sophomore year, we decided that Bill would move to Walla Walla on his own to begin his new job in December, while Will, my daughter, Sarah, and I would pack up the house and join him in June when school was out. Sarah was in the midst of planning her May wedding to her fiancé, Brandon, who, just weeks after the wedding, would be deployed to Korea with the U.S. Air Force.

In Montana, every winter I started seedlings under lights in my basement to transplant into my garden after the danger of frost was past (which in our part of the state could be anywhere from May to late June). Gardening in the higher elevations of Montana had its challenges! One year I started six hundred seedlings, which attested more to my plant greed than to any proficiency in my garden planning. I planted everything from bee balm to basil, carnations to columbine, dahlias to dianthus, four-o'clocks to foxglove, lemon balm to lavender, pansies to poppies, roses to rudbeckia, sweet William to sweet woodruff, and everything in between. This year I would be forgoing the winter tradition of planting seeds in lieu of packing.

Some of the plants in our garden held special meaning for us, so we decided that when Bill came to the wedding in May, he would take back a trunkful with him to transplant into the rich soil surrounding the 1950s ranch-style home he had found for us on a third of an acre in Walla Walla just inside of the city limits.

The last month before leaving Montana was a whirlwind of activity—full-time work, packing, tending the gardens, spending time with family and friends, Sarah's wedding, and showing the house to prospective buyers. Fortunately, the first people who looked at our home bought it. The young wife was a cook who was especially interested in the herb gardens. Our plum and apple trees and the perennial gardens surrounding the house were in full spring bloom, which certainly added to the property's appeal.

I spent the first year in Walla Walla weathering various stages of transplant shock. The surrounding countryside reminded me of the southeastern part of Montana where I had grown up, and this helped me acclimate to our new surroundings. The flowering variegated dogwood tree in our front yard was beautiful that autumn, displaying deep maroon and cream leaves and bright red berries that the birds feasted on. The existing rosebushes, which were still blooming in October, made a striking contrast against the autumnal colors of the deciduous trees.

The foggy winter appealed to my Celtic nature, so the gray months were not as depressing to me as they were to many of the local residents. I hunkered down in front of our little fireplace with our Westie, Jake, reading gardening books and discovering plants that would grow in our new zone 5–6 garden. On our first Christmas Eve in Walla Walla, we were surprised with a pile of snow that had been dumped onto our front porch by some of Will's friends who had gone to the mountains to bring it to us (via a cooler), knowing we were missing snow in Montana for the holidays.

When spring arrived, the plethora of white blossoms that covered the dogwood were as resplendent as a new bride, and the fragrance of neighboring magnolias, wisteria, and other blooming trees and bushes literally scented the air. I had a "scentual" glimpse of Eden via the olfactory nerves that I had never experienced anywhere else. Just a walk through the neighborhood was a feast for all five senses.

But the best welcoming committee of all that first spring were all of my transplanted Montana plants that carried special memories of family and friends. There was the wild columbine transplanted from Jackie and Dad's ranch; Cathie's white and red roses from Belgrade; Beth's four-o'clocks from Billings; Annie's miniature white roses given as a gift when visiting from Kenya; hollyhock seed from my sister Becky's garden, sown the previous autumn, that had already taken root; seed sprouting from April's Star of the Veldt. The merging of our Montana transplants with the existing garden surrounding our new home gave us a sense of continuity and harmony, and helped alleviate my homesickness.

We've been living in this beautiful valley for five years now, experiencing the charms of the "town so nice, they named it twice." I try not to gloat too much when Montana gardening friends call to say it's snowing, and I am still cutting roses in late October. I think this coming spring I'll try my hand at growing that elusive Himalayan blue poppy. . . .

# Memory Gardens

# Family and the Pumpkin Patch

*By Danita Cahill*

One late spring, when my daughter Alyssa was a first-grader, I planted a couple of extra hills of pumpkins, thinking she and I could enjoy some fun activities together when the pumpkins were ready. Little did I know then that besides providing mother-daughter bonding opportunities, the pumpkin patch would provide story fodder for my brothers for years to come.

While the vines were growing, Alyssa and I daily strolled hand in hand to the garden to check the pumpkins for progress. We watched as the golf ball–size fruits grew, swelled, and finally turned orange.

In early October, she and I harvested the pumpkins. I let her help decide where we should arrange them for autumn decorations. We tied clumps of tall cornstalks to fence posts behind each pile of pumpkins and topped the piles off with a few colorful gourds. We were happy with the festive autumn look. Later that month, I let Alyssa pick which pumpkins we'd carve into funny-faced jack-o'-lanterns. The rest she and I chunked up, boiled, peeled, pureed, and carefully measured into freezer bags to use for holiday baking.

The day before Thanksgiving, I pulled a couple of bags of the puree out of the freezer to thaw. Thanksgiving morning I was out of bed early to prepare pies and get them in and out of the oven before we headed to my folks' house for dinner.

"Mommy," Alyssa asked as I was scooping together the ingredients for piecrust, "can I visit with Kendra through the fence?"

"Okay," I murmured, up to my elbows in flour. I watched out the kitchen window as my daughter skipped across the north field to visit with her young friend on the other side. The skirt of her blue and white dress bounced with each step. She looked so sweet and carefree. Still, I sighed, imagining all the burrs I'd have to pick out of her kneesocks when she got back home.

I was rolling out the piecrust when Alyssa and her friend burst through the back door. "Guess what?" Alyssa announced. "Kendra's mom said she could come over for an hour."

I sighed again, thinking my daughter should have consulted me before inviting a friend over. It was Thanksgiving. I was busy. I didn't have time to run a day-care center. But it was a holiday, after all, and I decided to make the best of it—I put the girls to work. I found out the hard way that it's not easy to supervise two six-year-old bakers while in the midst of rolling out pie dough.

I tried to be a good overseer as the girls measured the spices. Somewhat patiently, I picked out the chips of eggshell after they cracked the eggs. They whisked the beaten eggs and canned milk together with the pumpkin. I poured the mixture into the finished shells and popped the pies into the oven.

Soon the ginger-spice fragrance of baking pies filled our kitchen. When a knife inserted in the centers came out clean, I pulled the pies from the oven. They turned out fine—or so I thought at the time—great smell, good color, the texture seemed right, and I felt proud that we'd grown the pumpkins ourselves.

I shooed the neighbor girl back across the field, picked the burrs out of Alyssa's socks, and loaded her and the pies into our Thunderbird. We headed north to Mom and Dad's.

It was a big gathering, as usual, and after my extended family had digested the generous, traditional Thanksgiving meal, we brought out the desserts. Grandma had baked blackberry pie, my favorite, so I opted for a slice of that, while my mom, aunt, and three brothers each dished up a piece of Alyssa's and my home-grown pumpkin pie.

We all plopped on some whipped topping and dug in.

Grandma's blackberry pie was heaven. And Mom and Auntie didn't moan, groan, or make faces while eating the pumpkin. Looking back on it now, I can't believe my brothers ate their slices without complaint either.

On our way home that afternoon, for who knows whatever reason, I ran the earlier pie assembly through my mind—the egg beating, the milk pouring, the spice measuring. But . . . what about the sugar?

My memory blipped at that point.

This blip settled into a brain hollow and haunted me for the rest of the forty-five-minute drive from my folks' house to mine. I didn't have a cell phone back then, but as soon as I got inside the door, I called Mom on my landline.

The conversation went something like this: "Uh, Mom, did you notice anything weird about the pumpkin pie?"

"Well . . . not really," Mom said. She was always mindful of others' feelings, sometimes almost too kind. "Why?"

"Because I'm not sure your granddaughter and her friend put in any sugar." Yeah, yeah. Let's blame this one on the kids, shall we?

"Now that you mention it, the pie wasn't very sweet." There was a hesitation on Mom's end. "I thought maybe you were try- ing a new recipe."

A dessert recipe without sweetener? Interesting concept, Mom. "No." It was time for me to stand up and face the band. "I just plain forgot the sugar."

"It wasn't so bad," Mom hedged, "with lots of Cool Whip."

Good old Mom.

My brothers, on the other hand, still give me a hard time about my baking skills, or, I should say, my lack thereof. For Pete's sake—it was four pies. One mistake. Years ago. But brothers, bless their boyish hearts, are not moms. Brothers thrive on family stories they can really sink their tease into.

# Mustard Greens— More Than a Pretty Almaden Valley Flower

*By Cookie Curci*

For many years, my Italian American grandparents worked the Almaden Valley land; they have been prune ranchers, cherry growers, farmers, and cannery workers. The cuisine they prepared and enjoyed was essentially food grown on their land. Some of their traditional foods came from the hills and orchards that surrounded the valley. Much of what they harvested they ate or preserved. Olives were cured for eating and pressed for oil, the oil was used for cooking and to preserve dried pork sausages, tomatoes were dried in the valley sun, and the deep green leaves of the mustard greens were gathered at the peak of the season as a tasty main course.

Longtime valley residents are familiar with the picturesque yellow flowers of the mustard green and how it once grew so plentifully in our fruit orchards and along the hillsides. They remember how it graced the orchard lands as a beautiful ground cover and how it painted our landscape with glorious, bright, sun-colored blossoms.

For those who enjoyed eating them, the pungent mustard greens were a fresh source of vitamin A. Valley ranchers generously allowed residents onto their land to pick the cherished greens. After a spring rain, my family and I were among the many mustard green enthusiasts to beat a path to the muddy orchards to gather our share of the bitter greens.

Another free-growing food was the wild quince that grew in the foothills surrounding the valley. Every year, Mom trekked to the area to pick baskets of the sweet, green fruit to make her jelly. Mushroom hunting was another all-day pastime that took us to the edges of the valley in our search for huge-growing tree mushrooms. Tall trees also sprouted bushels of mistletoe in December and January.

"Hunting" for a good mustard green patch takes plenty of skill and know-how. The greens have to be picked at just the right stage of development. Once the blossoms appear, the greens are no longer edible.

I can remember how local families would gather together early in the morning; clad in knee-high galoshes and bundled in warm clothing, we'd spend hours picking our favorite springtime greens.

After an exhausting morning of gathering the mustard greens, the tired, but contented crew of pickers returned home, our baskets and bags filled to the brim with greens and our shoes and boots covered in a thick layer of orchard mud.

Once we got home, we turned our kitchens into a process factory. Huge kettles were set on the stove; the mustard greens were washed in the sink to make sure all traces of the orchard mud were removed. Then the greens were cleaned and cut and placed into a pot of boiling water. The boiled greens were drained and then sautéed in olive oil, garlic, and dried red pepper. The aroma was heavenly, at least to an Italian kid like me, who loves mustard greens prepared Italian style. The remaining greens were boiled and frozen for another dinner.

On Sundays, when the family gathered at Grandma's house, the joyful fragrances of freshly cooked mustard greens and simmering tomato sauce permeated the atmosphere. On these occasions we waited anxiously to hear Grandma call out our favorite words, "Veini a mangiare." Before dinner was served, glasses of red wine were raised to our good health, along with Papa's celebratory words, "Salute per cent'anni."

"Good health for a hundred years," the family would echo back. Then, and only then, could the meal begin.

Today, sad to say, fewer and fewer families continue the Sunday dinner ritual. The plentiful prune ranches that once graced our valley and offered local residents free and bountiful greens have all but disappeared now. The 1960s and 1970s brought microwave cooking to the family kitchen, and a full-course dinner is being zapped in shorter time than it takes to swallow a predinner cocktail. The bright golden-yellow mustard green flowers that once filled our valley's hillsides and orchards are seen now only in sparse patches along the freeways.

The traditional foods from our past are getting harder and harder to find. My "hunt" for mustard greens, fava beans, and quince takes me to the corner supermarket, where, nine times out of ten, I'll not find them.

Recently, two longtime friends of mine braved the cold weather and muddy orchards to search out a small patch of mustard greens growing in an open field off the busy highway. My friends generously gifted my household with a lovely bundle of these freshly picked greens.

A pot of water was quickly set to boil. A few minutes later, the mustard greens were tossed into my frying pan with a little olive oil, garlic (of course), and dried red peppers. A loaf of French bread was torn into chunks, glasses of Chianti poured, and as we raised our glasses in a toast, we happily declared, "Salute per cent'anni!"

How comforting to know that good friends, traditional foods, and the flavors of our heritage can still be found—perhaps not in the same abundance as we once knew them, but still here for us to enjoy nonetheless.

# Honey, the Oregano Got Out Again!

*By Christine E. Collier*

I love colonial villages. The old buildings filled with charming antiques and casual atmosphere intrigue me. I'm talking about restored villages that transport you back in time a few hundred years or so. I love many things about them, but nothing appeals to me more than the herb gardens outside a quaint kitchen door enclosed in a white picket fence.

Years ago I decided to add a kitchen garden to my already flourishing lily and perennial flower garden. The new portion would be off my deck, which is outside my kitchen back door; thus, a kitchen garden. Close enough! I have a ranch-style house built in the '70s—1970s, that is. I didn't have a white picket fence with a swinging gate either, but that didn't matter. I was going to harvest fresh herbs for my family!

It was fortunate that a family-owned greenhouse was just a couple of miles away. My adventure began. Little containers of herbs were lined up in the old stone greenhouse. The gurgling sound of water and the musty smell of damp soil gave browsers that wonderful greenhouse experience. What should I buy?

Chives? Yes, indeed, my family loves chives smothered in sour cream on baked potatoes. Mint? Oh my, yes, I'd have fresh mint with our next leg of lamb, and what about those mint juleps? We might have one every fifty or sixty years or certainly the next time we watched the Kentucky Derby! Basil? Oh so good simmered in hot chicken noodle soup. Oregano? My mother always added oregano to her homemade pizzas and spaghetti sauce. I must have a container of that!

I planted the oregano in the corner, just a step from the deck. I might need some on a cold winter's night and not want to travel far. The other herbs were close by. The dirt in my garden is desert-like—the exact opposite of rich, fertile soil—lots of rocks and more than a touch of clay.

The oregano seemed to thrive, though, and took off growing faster than all the other herbs combined. The first summer it grew like the proverbial wildfire. I picked some to dry. No wasting money in the spice aisle at the grocery store for me!

I had three teenagers and a busy life when my garden addiction first hit. I was constantly driving one of them someplace or the other. My garden was my peaceful retreat.

"Mom, why are there weeds on the counter?"

"It's oregano and other herbs. I'm drying them to cook with."

"I'll pass on that, Mom! They look exactly like the grass that's clogged in the lawn mower. How do you know it won't kill us?"

"Our ancestors used herbs all the time, for many purposes. They even used it for medicine."

"Mom, they weren't in their right minds; they used herbs for medicine!"

I gathered big bunches of oregano, tied them with raffia, and hung them from the kitchen beams alongside my basket collection. Also, when the plants went to flower, I made a lovely oregano wreath. How could I get any more clever?

The oregano continued to spread. My husband started commenting when he mowed around the border of the garden. "Boy, that oregano is doing well, isn't it, honey?"

"It sure is!" I said beaming.

As the years went by, my ideas for using the herbs did as well. The plant did have a pretty bloom, so I just let it flower. My original garden had grass and weeds sneaking in faster than I could keep up. I made the decision to take up the stone paths and let it all go back to grass and start mowing again. I'd keep the herb garden portion, though.

The years flew by, grass got into the middle of the herbs as well, and the oregano had taken over the entire patch of herbs. I decided that the herb garden was to be mowed down as well. This made me sad, but it wasn't a neat herb garden anymore; it was an unruly oregano patch. And every time I looked at it, I felt guilty for not weeding.

It's been years since the demise of my garden. Basically, I gave up on it, not the other way around. Gardens are an expression of where you are in your life. You start out with great enthusiasm, or else you'd never bother to dig up that first shovel of sod. You create and execute your dream, maintain, and then life seems to divert your interests elsewhere. But isn't this true of most things in life?

The ghostly oregano remains, even though it gets mowed with each grass cutting. A carpet of little oregano plants live on, just as you step back from the deck. You can't kill it, and it actually has the final victory over the grass. The legacy of my garden lives on.

If you have terrible soil and want to harvest enough oregano for an Italian restaurant, invest in a plant or two. Be careful, though—some night you may hear your spouse yell, "Honey, the oregano got out again." I'm glad I did.

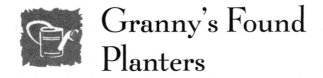

# Granny's Found Planters

*By Nancy Edwards Johnson*

"That flower bed could be put to better use by planting corn and beans," my grandpa would declare. My granny always tut-tutted and planted her flower seeds anyway. To her way of thinking, vegetables fed the stomach, but blooming flowers fed the soul. Granny loved flowers, but Grandpa failed to see the value in working so hard for anything not meant for the table.

Granny grew up and reared her family in the foothills of the Blue Ridge. Living isolated from friends and neighbors, and with no small towns or jobs around, they learned to make do. Granny learned early in life to value the simple things: squash blooms, zinnias, and even morning glories fresh with dew climbing the sugar corn. She knew how to squeeze every cent for all it was worth, and she knew how to squeeze every ounce of good from all her possessions. In her day recycling was not the fashionable thing to do, but a way of life.

Granny's pleasure in her garden brought her other sources of enjoyment. Hummingbirds flocked around her place. I've heard my daddy speak of seeing twenty or more gathered around

Granny's hollyhocks, flitting in and out among blooms as high as a man's head.

In Granny's day, no one went to a greenhouse to buy plants. The women shared flower bulbs and seeds with their friends and family. One would swap a few seeds from her marigolds with another for a little slip from a geranium she had held over for years. Everyone had flower gardens, and no one spent precious money on things some considered unessential to survive.

Many is the time we visited Granny and she'd show us some little sprig of a plant stuck in a Mason jar and placed on the windowsill in the sun. She'd hold it up and point proudly through the clear glass at tiny roots just starting to form. Her face would be aglow with the pride and happiness that starting a new plant brings.

Once roots sprang from the base of the cutting and grew out a couple of inches long, she'd shift the little plantlet into a tin coffee can. When her new treasure grew to survival size, she transplanted it into her flower garden.

Every little spot in her side yard was a kaleidoscope of visual delight. Each spring a procession of crocus, daffodils, tulips, and iris (she called them blue flags) paraded beside her green grass. With the first warm days of spring, golden candlestick (forsythia) burst into flower. Soon after, bloom-laden limbs of baby rambler (spirea, as we know it today) made snowy arches across her paths, and lilac bushes perfumed the air with their heavy, tantalizing sweetness.

When we visited Granny, she delighted in showing off her latest blooms. I loved running through her yard, thrilled by all her treasures, as much as she loved showing them off.

"See, I found me another tin can so I could plant my moss," Granny would grin. Velvetlike moss would be spilling down the sides of the rusty tin.

Along Granny's side yard and back door, she placed every old pot and container she could find. Here she planted her tiny rooted starts of decorative peppers, geraniums, and what she called firethorns. They glowed radiantly red when the days of autumn came. Her combination of barn fertilizer and loving hands could entice the most reluctant plants to bloom.

I first realized how thrifty and ingenious Granny was when I was six and the June roses were in bloom. Granny fixed supper for our family. When the meal was over, she heated a pan of dishwater on her iron woodstove. She'd used that same chipped and dented enamel pan as far back as I could remember.

That night as the water heated, something sizzled, and a small droplet of water shot from beneath the pan. It danced across the hot stove top. Before the first drop disappeared in steamy vapor, a second droplet followed. Pretty soon, an entire line of droplets marched across the stovetop and then sizzled into oblivion. I watched, spellbound.

Granny noticed my amazement. "My old dishpan finally sprung a leak." She shook her head and tut-tutted, clearly upset. Yet she carried the pan of hot water to the table and finished the dishes, swiping the small puddles of water collecting on the oilcloth.

With dishes done and the pan dried, she fetched a clean white rag and tore off a narrow strip. I watched, fascinated, as she tied a hard knot in one end. Then, in front of my unbelieving eyes, she found the hole and poked an awl through the tin. She placed the strip of rag over the hole and punched it through. Pulling the knot securely against the pan, she formed her patch. "There, that'll hold a little longer, maybe until I can get a new one."

A few months later the hole outgrew the rag plug and the pan sputtered and sizzled again. Its dishwashing days at an end, Granny carried it out to her garden and filled it with a mix of rotted cow manure and woods dirt. Then she shook in some flower seed.

The next time I saw the pan, dozens of brilliant, roselike blooms spilled over its sides. Succulent stems blazed with flowers in shades of red, orange, yellow, and pink. "C" roses she called them. Those same tiny roselike portulaca blooms remain one of my favorite flowers today.

When Grandpa wore his boots out, Granny found another use for them. She planted a colony of hens and chicks, which happily crept rosettes of clustered leaves over the sides and down the slit where the shoelaces had been.

Such reuse of "found" containers has almost become a lost art. But every so often I'll see unusual ideas for planting flowers and I'll remember Granny with a smile. One person I know boasts a child's rusty red wagon, the bed filled with the same succulent hens and chicks Granny planted in Grandpa's boots. With the wagon filled out thick and full, it makes a living coffee table that can be moved around.

I'm amazed when I compare the thrifty lifestyle of Granny's day to the spend-happy ways of today. None of the barrage of containers and planters available at local garden centers comes close to the built-in charm of Granny's found planters: her beloved dishpans, boots, and tin cans.

I wonder if these brand-new planters, sleek and beautiful as they are, will live in the memories of others and bring the same joy that Granny's found planters have always given me.

# Grandmother's Flowers

*By Shirley Dunn Perry*

My grammy Stella was the fastest blueberry picker in Grey-wood. She was also the one whom people ran to when someone was hurt or wanted to know the weather. Sometimes neighbors stopped in just to hear her stories. She was a backwoods woman, and she had the sight. Her garden was all the wildflowers that grew around her house and community: roses, daisies, asters, chicory, dandelions, and hundreds more.

Grammy told me about everything. What the crow said. When the rain was coming before there was a cloud in the sky. How to put spiderwebs on cuts that wouldn't stop bleeding. She talked to me like I was a grown-up, not some kid who should be quiet.

We'd go blueberry picking, and Grammy always knew where the best berries were. We'd walk up in the pasture, and all of a sudden she'd stop, her head would turn to the left or right, and then she'd take off. She never got out of sight, but she was following a trail that I couldn't see.

I carried a small lard can with a handle. It was shiny, and the sun reflected on it like a mirror. Grammy took two large galvanized water buckets. She'd call out to me, "Keep picking," when she saw me lying on the grass, blueberry juice all over my face. In the end though, she helped me fill my can, rounding it off at the top so it shone like a blue light.

Walking home was a long way. My can was heavy but I didn't mind. I was proud of my full can of berries and my grammy.

When we got to her house she'd put the kettle on to make tea. I drank water and ate one of her soft and gingery molasses cookies. I could only eat one, as they were the size of a small plate.

In the spring I always picked violets and mayflowers. They smelled sweet. I was careful not to break the stems too close to the flower heads as Grammy had taught me. With her rough hands, she'd tie a little string around their stems and put them in a glass of water. The way she touched and looked at those flowers made my heart beat soft and gentle.

I didn't go to her funeral. I had moved far away and was too busy. I had walked out of the backwoods thinking I wanted sophistication. I hadn't seen her for years, and the last time I saw her she didn't seem to recognize me.

In my prayers now, I send her flowers—big, white calla lilies. I see her take them tenderly. I feel her love and forgiveness for me. I sense her blessings. With each flower I gaze at, I send her thanks.

# Grandpa's Garden

*By Linda O'Connell*

Along with a healthy crop of tomatoes and peppers, one season compassion grew in my husband's garden.

After our children grew up and married, we moved into a condo. When our grandchildren started arriving, we purchased a small ranch house with an even smaller backyard. Although we gave up the luxury of a community pool, we absolutely felt like we had traded up. We were thrilled with the six-by-fifteen-foot patch of rich, dark soil at the far corner of our backyard. Bill had his idea of gardening, and I had mine. We couldn't wait to get our hands in the dirt. He had grandiose visions of a garden boasting the reddest, roundest, and plumpest tomatoes and crunchy green and yellow peppers. He even generously planted a few extra tomato bushes for the wildlife and neighbors. I envisioned my garden as a small artist's palette of petunias, marigolds, and minia-ture rosebushes—just a strip of soil along the perimeter of the patio. It was very satisfying planting, nurturing, and watching our gardens grow.

When the tomatoes and peppers were ripe, our grandchildren couldn't wait to help Grandpa pick his veggies. Kyle, then three, nibbled as many elongated banana peppers as he picked, and Ashley, then seven, harvested tomatoes until they overflowed the crook in her arm. They ate ripe, red, juicy tomatoes as if they were apples. Forget the toy box in the guest room. The kids were anxious to get into Grandpa's garden every time they came for a visit that first summer. Bill showed them how to walk on the stepping-stones between the rows, and he taught them about roots and shoots, leaves and stems. Every visit was a hands-on, fingers-in-the-soil nature lesson when they came to our house. "We love it in Grandpa's garden," they both said. They loved the dirt, the worms, and the buried treasure they discovered.

One late fall day, they came for a visit and ran out the back door. They stopped abruptly in their tracks. My flowers had all withered, and Grandpa's garden was barren; he had ripped out all of the plants. Devastated, they stood on the dry earth and cried, "Our garden!" Bill, a hulking six-foot-two, 250-pounder knelt down in the dirt beside the children. At their eye level, and with a gentle touch, he consoled them as he explained the life cycle of plants. He told them to expect a new crop next year, and he promised them that they could even help him plant in the spring.

In March, spring teased our town with a premature warm snap. Bill tilled the rich earth in his shirtsleeves in the hot sun; he was as anxious as the kids to dig in the dirt. He was wise enough to know that a frost would destroy a prematurely planted tomato crop. Each time Ashley and Kyle arrived, they'd plead with him to plant the garden. Together they counted the days until May 15, when they could plant again without the threat of frost.

The week before the scheduled planting, unexpectedly, Bill

had to have foot surgery and was incapacitated. The planting had to be delayed two more weeks. Patience is not a child's virtue. So Grandpa gave them permission to go dig in his garden when they came to visit. I handed each of them a big soup spoon, and they happily darted outside. Every now and then they came in to share a treasure they had unearthed. Then they'd rush back to the garden for more fun. This went on for more than an hour; the adults were content to stay inside while the kids happily played outside. The last time they came in, they lingered in the guest room for a little longer than usual, then they slipped out the back door unnoticed for more fun in Grandpa's garden.

When I peeked out the kitchen window to check on them, I gasped. Ashley and Kyle were tromping though the plot of dirt, bent over, each of them digging and planting. There were hundreds of flowers in full bloom, an array in every color and in every variety imaginable. A rainbow of flowers blanketed more than two-thirds of Grandpa's garden and they were still at it!

"Bill, come quick! You have to see this." He hobbled to the window and chuckled loudly.

"What are you kids doing?" he called.

"We're helping you, Paw-Paw, 'cause your foot's hurt," Kyle said.

"Yeah, Grandpa, we're planting your garden for you!" Ashley exclaimed proudly.

I soon discovered what they had discovered in the guest room. They had sneaked outside with my shopping bag, which was filled with an assortment of artificial flowers. I had intended to use them with my preschool classes for a combined science and arts and crafts project. Bill and I laughed with delight at the brilliant crazy quilt of fake flowers they had stuck in the dirt, a compassionate gift intended for their recuperating grandpa.

The grandchildren, now fifteen and eighteen, fondly remember playing "Grandpa's Garden." Kyle grows his own tomatoes and peppers each summer, and eighteen-year-old Ashley still has an affinity for pastel flowers—only now they come from her boyfriend. Thanks to Grandpa's garden, they both developed a deep appreciation for the good earth and what it can produce. One very special grandpa planted the seeds of love that sprouted a crop of compassion.

# Looking Out

*By Marilyn K. Eudaly*

I stood on the backyard deck looking out at the flowers Dad had planted and the place where his vegetable garden had been. Now grown up in grass, the garden was gone and so was Dad. Alzheimer's took his ability to plow and plant some years before. Months ago, the mind-altering disease took his life. My sister, brother, and I returned to remove his worldly possessions from the home he had shared with his third wife.

Dad had married again in his sixties. He and his wife had agreed that the possessions they brought into the marriage would go to their respective children when they died. Seven months after his passing, my siblings and I were back together. My brother traveled from east to west. I returned from the south to the north, to join our sister who still lived in our hometown. She had become, by default of location, the executor of the estate. The responsibility fell on her to make the arrangements, attend the memorial for the World War II veterans, and handle the paperwork. All that remained was to finish the process of closing out Dad's life.

Dad was a member of the "Greatest Generation." He is immortalized in the Naval Museum in Washington, D.C. He died at a time when many tributes were being made to all those who had served our country. I felt some guilt for choosing not to attend many of the memorials. Time and distance were often the deciding factors. His wife and his other daughter attended as many as they could. Although the memorials were wonderful tributes that brought honor to our father, they elongated the grieving and letting-go process.

This task, to remove his belongings from his last home, was more emotional than I anticipated. We experienced his life through things he saved, remembered events long behind us. We found unexpected items from our childhood. Boxes of mementos and household items from his life with our mother, his first wife, were stored in the basement. Emotions boiled up inside me. I sought a moment of solitude on the back deck.

I could not escape the memories of Dad. The flowers planted along the fence still bloomed. His barbecue grill and smoker still gave out the aroma of the meat he cooked. I could almost taste his special homemade barbecue sauce. There on the northeast corner of the backyard was where he planted his garden every year, just as his father had taught him.

Grandpa taught Dad by having him help in the garden. A garden was a necessity. Dad was one of thirteen kids, and the produce was needed to feed the tribe. The men worked the garden; the women preserved the food. Men did outside work; women worked inside. That was how life was in the 1920s and '30s.

Looking out at the spot where the garden had been, I recalled the wonder I felt when Dad showed my brother and me how to dig out the peanuts in Grandpa's garden. How proud they both were of being able to grow peanuts in a northern climate. Grandpa taught Dad, and Dad would teach me.

Well, Dad tried to teach me. It didn't take, partly because I was a girl. After all, men's domain was outside, and women's was inside. And I admit, much to Dad's chagrin, I was just plain clumsy among his flowers and vegetables. He almost cried when I pulled the plants along with the weeds. I almost cried when he harshly corrected my mistakes. I wanted to spend time with Dad, but alas, I was banished into the house to take my place with the womenfolk.

The pride he took in his garden and his accomplishments were things I didn't truly appreciate as a child. Standing on the deck he built, I looked out and realized the many life lessons Dad taught through his gardening.

There was the yearly contest to see who in the family grew the earliest, biggest, or best-tasting tomato. Dad would champion his tomato-growing skills against anyone's. He kept close watch as tomatoes grew red on the vine, always with hope one would ripen before the Fourth of July. There was a particular uncle he wanted to beat with the first vine-ripened tomato of the season. Some years he was the victor; sometimes he went down in defeat. Through these contests, he taught me how to accept victory and defeat graciously with good sportsmanship.

For Memorial Day, Dad cajoled the peonies to bloom just at the right time. Often I helped him pick the buds and refrigerate them, so they wouldn't open too early. Or I watched as he nurtured them so they would bloom in time. He often spoke of the importance of planting flowers along with the vegetables and fruits. Flowers added beauty and fragrance to enjoy when the back ached from working the soil. As we decorated cemeteries, he showed me how to grieve and care for those we have loved and lost.

Dad also grieved the death of his longtime nemesis, the groundhog with one missing toe due to Dad's trap. That groundhog mocked him to distraction on a yearly basis, along with the constant struggle to keep the rabbits at bay—not to mention the deer, squirrels, birds, and an occasional snake. Dad demonstrated the need, in the face of all adversity, to laugh at one's self.

He took pride in his accomplishments and accepted his defeats. I remain clumsy with plants of any kind. Still, Dad taught me well. From the deck I see three volunteer tomato plants that have sprung up. There is a rabbit that squeezed under the fence into Dad's once-upon-a-time garden spot and sat munching on something scavenged. I realize that this yard, once his domain, is the best memorial of all. I look out, and now I see the true legacy Dad left to me.

# Feeding the Soul

# Valentines in the Garden

*By Linda E. Allen*

Hearts—the universal symbol of love and Valentine's Day. From the ones pumping in our bodies to the man-made representations in our culture, the heart is so ever-present it has become a symbolic part of our alphabet, possibly the twenty-seventh letter. Emblazoned on buttons, T-shirts, coffee mugs, and bumper stickers, the bright red symbol proclaims our love for everyone and everything from Mom to skydiving.

But hearts aren't always red or available only on Valentine's Day or other romantic occasions. Have you ever wandered through a garden, forest, or a field of wildflowers and noticed love messages tucked among the beauty and fragrance of the flowers and plants? Plants with heart-shaped leaves and flowers in a variety of colors, patterns, shapes, and sizes are everywhere—God's "love notes" to us!

My family tree boasts many members with green thumbs who like to play and dig in the dirt. From my great-grandfather, grandmother, and mother, I learned the secrets of seeds and soil, folklore and flower legends. Many happy childhood hours spent in the garden have led to a lifelong love affair with all green, growing things. It seems I have always been busy in the garden, planting seeds, pulling weeds, watering, and fertilizing to nurture my plants to harvest time when I can collect and enjoy their fruits and blossoms.

With such longtime and intense involvement, you would think I am a careful and observant gardener, aware of both the major and minor events in my garden. Certainly, I am excited when seedlings first pop through the soil, annoyed when caterpillars and beetles use my garden as a salad bar, and thrilled when a flower or vegetable is just perfect for picking.

Through the years of concentration on my garden chores, I overlooked the most abundant and most obvious gifts of the garden, until one of those "aha" epiphany days of discovery when I noticed that many leaves and flower petals in my garden were shaped like hearts! From morning glories to moonflowers, my garden was filled with heart-shaped leaves and flowers. Roses, caladiums, hostas, impatiens, violets, geraniums, and ivy—that's just the short list. Scalloped leaves and petals like doilies, frilly ones in a rainbow of colors with striped or variegated colors, velvety or satiny—each is a personal "I love you" message from God.

Maybe I'm just a late bloomer. Oblivious to the obvious, I had hurried through my life, ignoring the truths that were often right in front of me. I was living the old adage about not seeing the forest for the trees and missing the natural beauty that surrounded me. In the beauty of my garden, I discovered mystical and spiritual messages from God. Instead of buried treasures in the soil, I discovered heart-to-heart communication that had been camouflaged by my busyness, worries, and preoccupations.

I realized God's presence speaks to each of us in the stillness and beauty of a garden with a rich bouquet of valentines, from elegant roses to lowly weeds. Take a walk through a garden, the woods, a field, or even a city park whenever you need a reminder or assurance of God's love. Stop and smell the roses—and all the other flowers—and look for God's valentines of love. He's always in the details and sometimes in the most unexpected ways! Happy Valentine's Day—every day—from God in the garden!

# Stephen's Garden

*By Jean Matthew Hall*

It is May again. My garden is bursting with color. Yellow daylilies yawn wide to capture the golden rays of sun. Pink Pentas and blue periwinkles dot the garden. Scarlet roses hang on curling canes that climb the trellis near my patio. Their sweet fragrance welcomes me to the yard as soon as I step out of the back door. My vegetable garden is gorgeously green and loaded with blooms, promises of tomatoes, cucumbers, squash, and melons to come. These luscious sights bring both joy and a tinge of sorrow—joy as I celebrate new life and spring, and sorrow as I remember another garden and another May.

In May 2001, our thirty-year-old son, Stephen, died suddenly of a heart attack. Memories of driving through the night to his home in Kentucky, arranging his funeral, and committing his body to the ground are blurry now. The heavy sadness we experienced at that time had a way of muddying the waters, of making the details hazy. I think that is a blessing, a small mercy that God gives us during a time of indescribable pain.

But one memory of that time is crystal clear. It is the memory of my little vegetable garden that awaited me back home. Six weeks or so before Stephen's death, I had planted my first vege-table patch. It wasn't even large enough to be called a garden: a row of tomato plants, a few squash, a couple of cucumber vines, and a few pathetic bell pepper plants. But that little vegetable patch got me through that summer of grief.

The evening we returned from Kentucky, I walked outside to inspect my little garden. I wasn't really interested in the plants, but in the solitude, I think. I saw the neglected plants and the weeds poking through the soil, and my heart was stirred. I couldn't take care of Stephen. I couldn't protect him from a heart attack. But I could take care of these helpless little plants. I stooped down and plucked some weeds from the soil.

So began my journey through grief. Every morning I sat on the patio for a few moments looking at my garden, praying, remem-bering Stephen, and absorbing the cool, peaceful quiet. Every afternoon I came home from work, prepared dinner and cleaned the kitchen, then headed straight for my garden.

Pulling weeds down on my knees put me in a natural posture for prayer. Running my hands through the cool soil and smelling the earthy fragrance were soothing to my spirit. I talked to God, to Stephen, to myself. I talked myself through the sadness of that summer.

In the solitude of my garden I could cry all I needed to with-out embarrassment. And I still had many tears left to cry that summer. While at work I tried to hold those tears in; why burden other people with my sorrow? I had a job to do, and they were at a loss for words to comfort me. But when I was alone in my gar-den, the tears could flow freely, washing away my grief.

That summer I pulled weeds, cultivated soil, discouraged insects, watered thirsty plants, fed struggling vegetables, and prayed for my garden. I mothered it. Inside my broken heart was a terrible need to mother someone. It couldn't be Stephen now. I desperately needed to nourish, to nurture along, to protect someone. My garden gave me that opportunity.

Babying those struggling plants was therapeutic for my soul. It was an outlet for my grief. It provided me with space and time to be quiet and to inhale the fragrant memories of my son. It let me "fix" something that was broken. That little garden kept me alive through sorrow so powerful I cannot describe it.

That summer my little vegetable patch didn't produce very many tomatoes or squash. It was barely worth the cost of putting it in the ground. But I do not know how I would have survived that time of sorrow without that little patch of ground and those pathetic plants. They needed me almost as much as I needed them.

I don't believe in "accidents." I believe that God knew back in February as I planned, and in March as I prepared, and in April as I planted, that I would desperately need that garden in May and June and July. And I believe that he knew the harvest I would really need to reap wouldn't be vegetables. I believe that months before Stephen's death, God lovingly prepared a way for me to work through some of my grief.

The Bible tells us that Jesus was "a man of sorrows, and acquainted with grief." Surely that applies to our Heavenly Father also—a father who knows the grief of watching his own son die.

I think I understand a little better now how he must have felt.

# Harvesting Hope, One Tomato at a Time

*By Maureen Helms Blake*

A gallon plastic bucket bulges with cherry tomatoes on my kitchen counter. I sit across the room in front of an open window, unseasonably warm autumn breezes blowing over me, and I wonder, *Can one apologize to a garden?*

Months earlier, I'd harbored little hope of a successful planting season when I barged ahead and stuck the sorry little sprouts in the ground. When I'd finally made it to the greenhouse, all that remained were loops and swirls of wayward growth with yellowing leaves and no identifying tags. The cheery clerk thought maybe they were cherry tomatoes, and wasn't I lucky I came today since they were throwing out all the leftover plants tomorrow and I could have two for the price of one if I wanted?

I took all she offered, despite the folly of planting in July in a state whose growing season is capricious. Some years I'd managed to pick just the right day, after a surprise spring snow or before summer temperatures surged. But had I missed the window of opportunity this time? Wet days and persistent gray kept me indoors most of June, mourning the likely loss of a summer garden. Finally the weather warmed. I bought the almost-tossed-out plants and set them on the deck. The next morning, after a rogue hailstorm, I surveyed the wreckage. I hadn't thought these plants could look any more pitiful. I was wrong. Some spindly vines had been stripped of their protective leaves, while others lost limbs.

Logic urged abandonment. Economy advised against wasted effort. But I dug in my heels. The plants couldn't even stand upright. What about sideways? Out in the garden I scooped out a home for each sprout, laying nearly a foot of stem and root horizontally across a trough, then smoothing over the dirt. Then I wrapped each with a newspaper collar to prevent cutworms from decapitating the plants, and to support the wavering stems, now at right angles to their roots.

As I gave the plants their first long drink, satisfaction soothed my tired muscles. I hadn't given up. Frost could rob me of any hearty harvest, but who knows? My summer's dream might still bear fruit—a hamburger grilled outdoors, topped with a tomato slab warm from the vine. As the plants started producing blossoms, though, that culinary vision faded. I could tell from the clusters that all my plants would, if they could at all, bear cherry tomatoes. I adjusted my expectations to imagine tiny fruit, sweet enough to eat like candy.

Soon, though, even this brief flowering of hope withered. Despite multitudes of yellow blossoms, not a single green tomato appeared. Discussions with local gardeners yielded no insight. One friend's plants hung heavy with fruit, while another's, a few streets over, stayed barren. Was it lack of pollination? Our sudden triple-digit heat? Whatever the cause, I felt helpless. When one, then two more hard green marbles finally appeared, gratitude softened the edges of my disappointment. If these hardy specimens matured, I'd enjoy a few bites of summer. In the meantime, I focused on the lush green growth, dotted with butter-yellow blossoms.

Despite daily visits to water, I must have lessened my diligent surveillance. Preoccupied with the impending end of a marriage that had lasted for more than thirty years, I no longer expected from the tomato plants what seemed impossible. Then one day, late in August, my eyes were opened. One cluster of tiny green globes caught my attention, then another, and another. I raced up and down, searching all nineteen plants, and found fruit everywhere. Within days, the green hues pinkened. And then, oh glory! One morning three red tomatoes dangled, begging to be eaten. I obliged, savoring the snap of their tender skin and the sweetly tart explosion.

Every day, the harvest increased. First a handful, then a brimming bowl. Then came the morning when I brought in an ice-cream pail half full, more than I could eat before the next gathering. I sorted and washed, then filled plastic bags for the freezer, dreaming of making tomato soup in the dead of winter, resurrecting summer if only for an evening.

A frost two weeks ago halted much of the flower gardens, but my sweet tomatoes seemed to take no notice. Today's gathering does not disappoint, and I lug the pail to the house, hoping its plastic handle doesn't break. Several hundred globes look ready to pick in a few more days, but hundreds more green ones will likely not make it past the next hard frost. I could uproot the plants and let them try to ripen in the garage, but something in me resists the thought of attempting to manipulate this brave tangle of gangly vines. They had persevered despite the wilting of my faith. Who am I to interfere now?

My stomach growls for supper. I think I'll eat a wedge of iceberg lettuce, drizzled with raspberry vinaigrette and surrounded by as many ruby tomatoes as the plate can hold. Throughout the coming winter, my garden will feed me, body and soul. And with each spoonful of soup, I will breathe a silent "thank you." Those scraggly, hail-smashed, nearly discarded plants ignored all inhospitable conditions and still bore fruit bountifully, even extravagantly. Maybe, just maybe, so can I.

# There's Gotta Be Dirt in Heaven

*By Loree Lough*

It's no surprise, really, that most of us love digging in the dirt with an aim toward making good things grow. It's been part of human DNA at least as far back as 650 BCE, when the Hanging Gardens started, well . . . hanging!

Aristotle's successor, Theophrastus, was one of the first to write about things botanical, laying the groundwork for future gardeners like Pliny the Elder and Pliny the Younger. Wealthy Egyptians and Romans alike grew gardens that sheltered them from the heat of the sun, and at Monticello, Thomas Jefferson left many of his neighbors green with envy as he produced perfect species of fruit, flowers, and vegetables.

My kids and grandkids have knelt beside me, learning lessons about science and nature and the abundant beauty that comes from an investment of time, patience, and tender loving care. Neighbors have shared cuttings with me, and I've passed my own to those who've spread the ripening wealth with others, carrying on a gardening tradition that's centuries old.

Arlo Guthrie, John Denver, and Carrie Jacobs-Bond have penned notes and lyrics praising the garden. Movie titles like *Midnight in the Garden of Good and Evil* and novels like *The Savage*

*Garden* were inspired by—you guessed it . . . a garden!

I've done my share of happy humming and plot-weaving while in my gardens. And, like my illustrious predecessors, I'm no stranger to broken fingernails and ground-in soil on my hands, knees, and clothing. And I'm sure that, like every famous gardener before me, pride in my hard-earned, sweaty filth is surpassed only by my proud preening over stellar sprigs and sprouts that are the direct result of my careful cultivations.

But over the years, what I've grown in my gardens pales in comparison to what I've taken from them. To be sure, aromatic blossoms and edible delicacies have gladdened me, my family, friends, and neighbors, but it's the peace and tranquillity found amid those dazzling colors and heavenly fragrances that draw me back day after day. Heart hurts and soul sorrows heal out there under the brilliant glow of the daystar! My worries are buried with every seed and root-ball, forgotten as I prune and pluck, trim and tuck; though my original goal might have been to bring about beautiful shapes and smells, gardening is the balm that cures my cares.

Some believe that God and his angels dwell on high, where cherubim dance and seraphim sing amid golden thrones and thick whiffs of white clouds, but I contend that heaven is where the Almighty and his minions go after they've labored alongside his faithful followers in gardens found around the world.

We humans started out in a garden, after all, so it's not so far-fetched to expect that when we draw our last breaths, we'll find ourselves surrounded by the simplicity and grace of a peaceful garden.

There's gotta be dirt in heaven, and I can't think of a more savory or satisfying end!

# Garden Sense

*By Jo Rae Johnson*

've always disliked getting dirty. I never made mud pies, nor was I an "outdoor" sort of girl. After all, have you ever seen a "Gardening Barbie" with a rake? My first home purchase came with a yard void of any color. A yard lacking flowers is like a white room without decor. Decorating I understood, so the gardening seed was planted and sprouted a new passion. I didn't realize there were lessons to be learned that had nothing to do with gardening and everything to do with living.

It's hard for me to describe the love I have for my garden. Discovering the first flower opening each spring is much like the birthing of a child. Only God knows the exact date and time the gift will be revealed. There is a unity of being part of something far greater than myself as I till the soil, preparing a fertile home for each new addition. My landscape diagram is pulled out and each plant chronicled. Its location, planting date, and the spectrums of color are duly noted. Planned symmetry found here is but a poor imitation of the perfection of a garden naturally planted by God.

In the stillness of early morning, dew glistens on the petals of each plant, flower, and blade of grass. The irrigation system clicks on and begins its synchronized dance with cascading streams of water moving left to right, following its program at the appointed time. The metered spray gracefully arches over plants that reach out with open mouths, like small birds being fed by their mother.

Weeds, daring to intrude into the carefully cultivated banks of color, are much like sin. I am reminded of how easily either can creep in and multiply if left unattended. I've found that while kneeling among the abundant trespassers, prayers are lifted up naturally, and along with them my burdens.

Dusk descends quietly and fireflies begin their dance, in and out of sight, pinpoints of light. The sounds of evening slow to the cadence of the porch swing. Creaking wood strains against supporting chain with each push of my foot. This is the time of day in which the garden gloves and clogs come off and the loveliness of each garden spot can be enjoyed.

I love the "tools of the trade." A basket of wildly colorful floral garden gloves that never release all their dirt, even after a washing, brighten my area of the garage. Hanging from their hooks are my spade and pruners, adorned with purple pansy-covered handles, easily found when dropped onto the grass. A straw hat with a white chiffon tie is a treasured gift from my children. Although much too pretty to wear while getting dirty, the hat looks lovely caught on the corner of my potting bench.

Seasonal gardening classes lure me with possibilities found in the newest cultivars. From azaleas to zinnias, the textures and colors of the garden beckon me from my seat. How I love taking copious notes, never again read, but carefully retained in my garden notebook.

How could I forget the smells? The earthy smell of mushroom compost mixed in the soil brings rich nutrients to baby plants much like Flintstone vitamins once did for my children. Lavender, when rubbed between my fingertips and brought to my nose, emits its calming aroma that some believe can bring sweet sleep. Gardenias always remind me of my grandmother with their old-fashioned scent reminiscent of perfumes popular long ago and cloyingly familiar.

Honeysuckle tastes as good as it smells and brings to mind the simplicity of my childhood. I still love to pinch off the stem's tip and slowly draw out the one drop of heavenly nectar found there, extending my tongue to catch it for a taste as sweet as honey.

The amazing daylily bloom, savored but a single day, reminds us to enjoy the present moment before another replaces it. But I am more like the rose, a high-maintenance flower needing much attention. If neglected, we are eaten up with infestation and begin to die a little each day. Given devoted and consistent care, the rose and I thrive and fully blossom with our God-given potential.

I love my garden because it reminds me to focus my senses on the splendor God has provided that so often goes unnoticed and unappreciated. Gardening has taught me patience as I wait to see what it will yield each season from my previous efforts. I've also discovered that there is a time to sit and reflect on the work of the day and to stop moving long enough to do just that.

Gardening, much like life, offers no reward without effort, and beauty is often found in the backyard of your own soul if you'll only look for it.

Enough pondering—I think I'll get back to the garden.

# Weed Wisdom

*By Ferida Wolff*

For all the time I spend in my garden, one would think that it would be manicured and pristine. It isn't. It is overrun with weeds. I pull them out and they return, half hidden among the stems of my flowers or cozily tucked into the fullness of a bush.

I could get angry about this situation except that I learn so much from weeds. It is like sitting at a master's feet every time I go into my garden. Weeds are remarkably flexible and have a variety of ways of claiming their turf.

Strawberries have established themselves in the back of the garden, letting their vines creep over the earth. The seeds must have come from the birds because I didn't plant them. I didn't find the shoots until they started to insinuate themselves in my iris bed. Now they are growing everywhere. While I love strawberries and wouldn't mind them growing in a contained area, if I let them continue to propagate, they will take over. From the irises, their vines have moved outward in focused straight lines, invading my lawn. I pull them but the leaves snap off while their vines remain, available to sprout again. They have a job to do and are exceedingly capable at it.

Clover is clever. It, too, spreads along the ground but with a whole different personality. I pull up one flower and it takes me on a trip in many directions. The runners follow a labyrinthine path that makes it almost impossible to find the main plant. They twist and turn, run over each other, and circle back, connecting and interacting with other plants along the way. This is extreme networking. I wish I were as good at this skill as the clover. It amuses me to think that I buy clover sprouts in the supermarket to eat but yank clover plants from my garden and toss them away.

Other weeds spread their seeds to establish new plants. Dandelions form tempting puffballs of delicate seeds that invite a child to blow on them. An adult is not immune to the allure. I certainly am not. Off they go with the slightest breath. The seeds scatter on their little helicopter blades to gardens all over the neighborhood.

There is a grass, I don't even know its name, that when touched shoots its seeds in all directions. I used to try to gather them up but there is no way I can find them all. Now I just hope I can find the plant before the seeds are ready to spring, though it seems to be a fool's task.

Am I as flexible as a weed? I wonder. When something comes along that could stop me from growing, can I find another way to express myself, another path to follow, a different way to flourish?

Weeds know the power of beauty. They send out lovely little flowers that I am reluctant to discard. How can such delicate beauty be bad in a garden? I received a packet of wildflower seeds in the mail. I would love to randomly disburse them in my garden and let them blossom into the gorgeous reds and golds, pinks and purples that are illustrated on the package. I think it will be too much, though. The individual flowers that I planted and love will be overlooked in the proliferation of wild seeds, as hard to notice as one person is in a crowd. I remember seeing a sign on a store window: "Too much is never enough." Maybe sometimes it is.

There is a life force in weeds that doesn't quit. Pull them out, and they will return. Try to eradicate them in one area and they will have their seeds hop a ride with a bird or animal and relocate to a different place. Decide they are ugly and they will morph into a variation that will be absolutely charming. Weeds are creative, if nothing else, when it comes to staying alive.

I once saw a dandelion poking out between the bricks on a path, sprouting through an unexpected late winter dusting of snow. It was the most arresting thing, this sudden burst of yellow, in the wrong season and the wrong place. Yet exactly for those reasons, it was truly an object of delight. No doubt that same dandelion would be plucked when spring came around, an unwanted nuisance. It made me think that anything can be a weed, even a daisy or a daffodil, a lily or a rose, if it is growing where it isn't wanted. A weed is just a seed that doesn't belong in the place where it happens to grow. It makes me think about the children who are born into families that can't care for them, children who are growing in the wrong place and struggling to survive. Weeds help me to keep in mind how precious life is in its many forms.

Of all the things that weeds teach me, however, what I most value is their persistence. They don't give up. Every day they work to get the nourishment they need. They find ways to live fully.

They keep expressing their unique characters, no matter the obstacles, as they reach for the sun.

I continue to weed my garden so that the other plants might grow, but I thank the weeds for sharing their wisdom with me. And for reminding me that I, too, no matter what life has in store for me, can keep reaching for the sun.

# Garden Variety

# The Patience of a Peony

*By Lisa Scott*

didn't know a delphinium from a dahlia until I moved into my first house. Luckily, my neighbor was a gardener. Her tiny city plot was packed with beautiful flowers, and the one that caught my eye was the showiest of them all: a Japanese tree peony, she told me. Its huge white flowers seemed too impossibly lovely to be real.

While my neighbor was kind enough to give me divisions of her plants to get me going on my new gardening hobby, she couldn't divide that tree peony. Those grow on a single woody stem. And with a tight flower budget, I wasn't going to spend fifty dollars on the tree peony I found at a local nursery. I would just enjoy hers next door.

Then I moved into a new home with big gardening plans, but I still couldn't justify the hefty cost of a small tree peony when I had so many other shrubs and flowers to buy. So I bought a few bare root tree peonies in a box marked down at the end of the season. Visions of the big showy flower danced in my head all winter long.

But only two came up the next year. I called the company, and they replaced the ones that hadn't survived. But they died on me again. The other two were so slow to grow, I didn't see a blossom for years. And the one bud I finally did see shriveled up. I figured the spot was too shady, so I moved the plant. And it died.

Was I just not destined to have the flower I'd coveted from the beginning of my gardening hobby? It only made me more determined to see one of those blossoms bobbing next to the columbine and irises.

So the next year I caved in and spent fifty dollars on a tree peony. It had evidence of a blossom just passed, so I was guaranteed at least one flower if not more the next year, right?

But, no. This spring, checking on my precious plant day after day, I realized it was not going to give me a blossom. I looked to the sky and laughed. Some things just aren't meant to be. Then, while surveying the rest of my garden, I checked on that one remaining tree peony from the box that I'd long ago given up on. It was developing a full bud, stretching to the sun.

I ran out there every morning like an expectant mother, waiting for the day it would open. I didn't even know what color it was going to be! What anticipation after so much disappointment. And finally, thirteen years after I first saw that gorgeous tree peony in my neighbor's backyard, I had one of my own blossoms to admire. Pale pink, and just as beautiful as I remembered.

I probably should have bought one from a nursery much sooner than I did. But looking around at my flower beds, I realized that even though that tree peony blossom may have taken a while to come into my life, it launched a love of flowers and skills I've honed over the years. It is the cherry that took forever to land on top of my sundae. And I savored each day it lasted, until a windstorm tore its petals apart and blew them away.

So I'll be waiting and watching next year. Maybe I'll find two blossoms. And maybe mine will be glorious enough to inspire a love of gardening in another newbie.

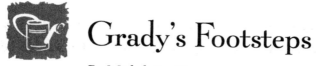

# Grady's Footsteps

*By Michele Ivy Davis*

*Lives of great men all remind us*
*We can make our lives sublime.*
*And departing leave behind us*
*Footsteps on the sands of time . . .*

—Longfellow

Many years ago, several miles outside of Washington, D.C., and only a few blocks off the main road to Frederick, Maryland, sat what was left of the crossroads community of Derwood. It consisted of a few old houses, two country churches, an abandoned rooming house/post office, and a lawn mower repair shop. There were no stores, no shopping centers, and no gas stations. Surrounding it on three sides were cornfields as far as the eye could see on our rolling countryside. On the fourth side, separating it from the rush and congestion of the highway northward, were the B&O Railroad tracks—straight guardians of Derwood's isolation and another way of life.

Grady and his wife lived in one of the old Victorian houses in Derwood. Each time our family rattled our way over the railroad's level crossing, we would see him working in his garden, his white hair gleaming in the sun. He was probably in his fifties, but no one knew for sure. His ruddy complexion and the wrinkles around his eyes could have come from age, working outdoors in the sunlight, or from smiling—yes, certainly from smiling.

One morning as I picked the first iris of spring, I thought about Grady and the many footsteps he left behind. I took the flower into my children's school, where I helped out from time to time.

"It's beautiful!"

"I've never seen anything like it!"

"Where did you get it?"

Exclamations. Questions. All about a single flower—one huge purple-blue iris, its deepness streaked with brilliant white. Surely, an expensive hybrid.

"I'm thinning my iris plants," Grady had said several years before, shortly after my husband and I had moved into our own ancient house not far away. "Want some?" And he proceeded to fill our car trunk with the healthy plants that bloomed each year with great velvet heads of yellow, brown, blue, and nearly black. Hundreds of dollars' worth of plants.

Most people would have sold them, but, no thank you, he wouldn't take payment. "Someone gave them to me," he said simply, "so I'm giving them to you."

Grady was like that. He was like the old section of Derwood— a part of a time when houses had porches for visiting, everyone knew everyone else, and if your neighbor needed help, why then, you helped him. It was as simple as that. He was known to take his tractor over on a stifling, hot day to help a friend he saw cutting his lawn with a hand mower, or take some firewood to an elderly neighbor and then spend the rest of the afternoon splitting it for him.

He was never in a hurry. If you wanted to stop by for a chat, that was fine. If you wanted him to check on something at your house, he'd do that, too. Not that he wasn't busy. He always had a project going and managed to get up earlier, work harder, and get twice as much done as those of us half his age.

My husband and I spent many fretful hours trying to keep up the repairs on our old house and cut the grass, but Grady seemed to do it with ease. His yard was the neatest and cleanest in the neighborhood. His lawn was always freshly mown, and in his huge vegetable garden, the rows were straight and frustratingly weed-free. He had land to clear, buildings to build, food to can, and a full-time job. But stop by his house and he'd greet you as if he had all the time in the world. Come in. Sit down. Something to drink?

Although he seemed at first meeting to be a man of few words—an observer—those who knew him soon found he was also a teller of tales. He worked as a handyman for the school system, and break time would find him with the others in the tiny room under the stairs, coffee cup in hand. There they would sit, draped over their school-issue wooden chairs, discussing the merits of black snakes or garden tillers with equal enthusiasm. Grady, his face poker serious and his eyes crinkling ever so slightly at the corners, would top any story anyone told at any time. Whatever it was, he had it, or knew where he could get it, bigger, cheaper, and in greater quantity than anyone else. The others would shake their heads or raise an eyebrow, but they listened. There were occasional disbelievers in the group, but they soon found, as the others had, that if they slyly checked up on his story, every word was the truth. It never failed. And it drove them crazy.

Ask him for advice, for help in growing things, and Grady became the teacher. How do you plant raspberries? When do you put in corn? Where can we order apple trees? Bees? He had several hives. Good for the garden. Here—you can keep one of my hives at your place. Onions? What do you mean you can't grow them? And he would reach down and pull up an onion bigger than anything I'd ever seen.

He seemed to know it all, and his patience was remarkable. Sometimes, though, I must admit, he would look at us quizzically, run his fingers through his snowy hair, and I could almost see him wondering how two full-grown adults could be so ignorant.

Then one warm October evening, the rescue squad came screaming through Derwood, and we got word that Grady had died of a heart attack. It was sudden, unexpected, and brutally final.

Abruptly, or so it seemed, things started to change. Within a year, the farms and cornfields surrounding Old Derwood were sold. Soon there were apartments, town houses, and single-family homes where the red-winged blackbird once flew. They closed the bumpy, teeth-rattling railroad crossing and built a smooth, four-lane bridge farther south; the new Metro high-speed trains that were coming were too fast and too dangerous to have level crossings anymore. Bulldozers filled the air with the musty odor of freshly turned earth, clearing the brush and trees for another set of parallel tracks for the new trains—tracks that would end in a huge station, storage yard, and parking for twenty-five hundred cars within sight of Grady's house. And in Derwood there was talk of who would sell, whose land would go commercial.

Sometimes progress just can't be stopped. Land that close to Washington, D.C., was suddenly too valuable for corn, and people had waited too many years for the Metro to get that far out. I knew that.

But seeing all of those changes coming made me afraid that maybe, just maybe, by not having to stop at the crossing (and count the freight cars and wave to the engineer), by tearing down the houses with front porches (and swings), we were going to lose forever the very essence of a time that was passing. It worried me, seeing that slip away. I wanted to say, "Wait! Stop for a minute! A whole way of life will be gone!" Smoothed over like wind-flattened desert sands.

Then I, who was brought up in a world of superhighways, convenience stores, and permanent press, noticed something. My children gobbled up their vegetables simply because we grew them in our own garden; we took great pleasure in giving away cuttings of the iris plants that were so freely given to us; and we viewed with pride our neat rows of canning jars sitting on the shelves, full and secure against another freezing winter.

I realized that although the physical structures were torn down and hauled away, everything wasn't gone. Grady, simply and unknowingly, had seen to that by leaving his mark in our lives and the lives of others—footsteps on the sands of time.

# Phabulous Gardens

*By Suzan Davis*

Yards can bring neighbors together or tear them apart. An otherwise unassuming patch of grass can divide smart men from smarter men. A fellow can stand at the highest point of his estate and look down onto his neighbor's yard to get a meter on how he can be measured as a man, as a really smart man.

Take Phil. His nickname is Phabulous Phil for a reason. His lofty IQ has reaped him steady and lucrative employment, allowing him to hire someone to mow his lawn for $130 a month at his Brookshire estate, while his wife, Fran, Fabulous Fran, plants seasonal flowers in full bloom. Their vibrant reds, oranges, and yellows jump right at you, in perfect rows. Fran never sneaks a peek at the price, while her next-door neighbor (me) hunts bargain-basement bulbs and settles for a few rough spots.

Phabulous Phil was reminded how smart he was one day when the male next door, otherwise known as Dennis (my husband), spent $150—without dickering—on a neighbor's riding lawn mower that wasn't much younger than he. Dennis quickly laid down seven twenties and a ten, so someone smart like Phil wouldn't come along and snatch up the keys.

Roaring like a lion over the Serengeti, the tractor/mower headed down East Carmel Drive, leaving a trail of smoke and some sort of eye-watering fragrance in its wake. At that very moment, Phil realized one more time just how smart he was. Dennis's new rig was silver. That was not the original color of the John Deere tractor/mower with grass catcher, but duct tape overpowered the original green.

"Phil just loves sitting out on the lawn chair and watching Dennis zip around the yard in that mower," says Fran. "He laughs and laughs, just waiting for it to fly apart around a turn."

"We haven't seen a mosquito since I bought that smoky beast," retorts Dennis.

One day, Phabulous Phil decided to upgrade his garden and ordered some kind of fancy dirt—called mulch—to be tossed into Fran's flower beds and around the tree trunks.

Tom, whose garden is located directly across the cul-de-sac from Phil's garden, had just been proclaimed "Brookshire Yard of the Week." A sign with a big castle announced this to the multitudes of cars that passed on Carmel Drive. Some whispered that this prompted Phil to invest in fancy dirt, but there is no proof.

Phil settled into his sea green lawn chair and smiled as Dennis flew past on the silver streak. As he heard the roar and whiffed the smoke intermingled with freshly cut grass, Phil opened his mail. The bill for the dirt and spreading it: $750.

The next morning a homemade sign in Phil's front yard broadcast, "Brookshire Mulch of the Month." Some suspect Dennis, though he denies it. For the price of dirt, he could have had five riding lawn mowers, but he's happy with one.

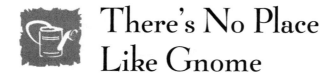

# There's No Place Like Gnome

*By Roberta Beach Jacobson*

tarting in late March or early April each year, whimsical creatures known as garden gnomes emerge from hibernation to decorate gardens throughout Europe. Gnomes have been likened to one or more of the Seven Dwarfs or to Santa's elves, but each gnome has a characteristic charm all his own—made all the more comical when he is observed standing guard over a patch of red and yellow tulips that tower over their little sentry.

Considered distant relatives to leprechauns, but unschooled in finding pots of gold, gnomes are more likely to encounter pots of dirt. Folklore has it that gnomes store treasures deep within the earth, though scientists have yet to uncover any evidence.

There are few rules in gnomedom, except that it remains male-dominated territory. Ceramic gnomes of yesteryear have given way to more modern plastic models. The wee folk (ten to twenty-four inches tall) usually sport droopy caps and most favor white or silver beards. Most are dressed in work clothes and often hold rakes, hoes, or buckets. Gnomes typically tend to carry a little extra bulk around the midsection, apparently due to their lack of exercise. Standing stationary in a petunia patch doesn't help anyone to work off those extra ounces.

The bigger the garden, the larger the gnome population—not! It's a matter of personal taste. Estate-size gardens may well have an "only gnome," while a postage stamp–size city garden could have half a dozen, complete with colorful cottages or barns.

Known as *Gartenzwerge* in German gardens or *nains de jardin* in French gardens, these proud little fellows may soon be on the endangered species list. An international group known as the Garden Gnomes' Liberation Front (FLNJ), headquartered in France, kidnaps gnomes from private gardens to "free" them in nearby forests. The notorious band has been operating primarily in the French regions of Alençon, Rennes, and Caen since 1996. Typically, gnomes are given new identities (in other words, repainted), so owners won't be able to recognize them. Whether the gnomes themselves actually desire to be set free is a matter of considerable debate among Europeans.

Europeans do seem to associate owning gnomes with having good luck, but that's only part of the draw. Traditionally, garden gnomes have been considered part of the family unit, much like a pampered pet. Owners boast that these low-maintenance fellows don't bark, won't claw the furniture, and will bite only if strongly provoked. Dog owners rarely own a gnome, for the obvious reason that Fido could easily mistake the little guy for a grinning fire hydrant.

Gardens should, after all, be fun and full of magic. Perhaps you've been charmed by these wee garden folk yourself and are considering opening your heart to a garden gnome or two during your upcoming European travels. They can be adopted from gift shops or the garden section of most department stores starting at the equivalent of about €12 (about $15).

# Ultimate
# Garden Ties

*By Bobbe White*

Unless a flowering plant could sustain itself, it wouldn't have much chance of living in my garden.

Lack of water, attention, and time added up to the overall demise of my usual gardening efforts.

The mantra at our house became, "Never buy more flowers for the garden in the spring than you can water all summer."

I always did and, for some reason, could never keep up. I just wasn't committed or invested in the garden. This year, however, I realized that a garden was so much more than watering, weeding, and pruning.

Martha Stewart, I'm not. My garden IQ was very low. The weeds were terribly high, and our dog's digging left holes that were ridiculously deep.

And then, our neighbors professionally landscaped their adjacent garden. After all, the garden was so promising that it had been the major selling point of the home.

The neighbors entertained on their newly poured patio at an escalating rate. Meanwhile, my garden-consciousness plummeted. (Like self-consciousness, but more visually apparent to the neighbors.)

Every yard with overly mature trees, like ours, produces patches of barren ground. Nothing, I mean nothing, grows there. Except weeds, of course.

Gardening gloves, watering can, and a garden store gift card were presented to me on Mother's Day this year.

After my attempt to beautify the barren patch with fake, red geraniums, and a berating by my children, I spun into action.

Remedial gardening was my limit. I realized my learning curve for an average garden was steep. I extracted the weeds and applied the black weed mat that guaranteed new weeds would not appear in the near future.

Determination was my fuel. Mulch became my vice, to the tune of fifteen bags or more. I quit counting. I poked holes through the fabric and stuck and transplanted a few plants from other pots. I could sense Carol and Elias, my neighbors, observing my efforts.

Even the three sand dollar stepping-stones I'd purchased at an art show last year found a home among the mulch. My neighbors edged closer to see the progress and expressed appreciation at my lone effort to improve the view.

Next came the hurdle of how to edge my garden. Frustration set in when I realized how much square footage I'd created. The plastic edging I purchased screamed, "WALMART!" while the neighbor's professionally placed stone whispered, "Tiffany's." Elias recommended an inexpensive circular stone that would interlock with the next. They looked like little Pac Men, gobbling each other up, but a neat boundary row was achieved. The plastic edging was returned.

The neighbors offered to donate a few plants that they didn't need. In a short time, the transplants took hold; one of them even bloomed! I was delighted with my adopted, flourishing flowers.

In the end, several things grew: (1) the garden, of which I was as proud as a new mare fussing and fawning over her yearlings; (2) my self-esteem, because I realized I was capable—even though in an amateurish way—of tending a garden; and (3) a friendship with Carol and Elias.

Even as the garden season ends, the flowers have run their course, and the rabbits help themselves to green leaves, I feel proud as I look forward to grooming the garden for next year.

Somehow, it never occurred to me that an effort in the garden could open a gate to the soul.

# The Bird Lady's Pot

*By Nancy Edwards Johnson*

andy, my new helper, came running down the greenhouse aisle. "Will you help me? I've got a picky customer and I can't find a thing to please her."

The panicked look in her eyes worried me more than her words. "What's her problem?" I asked, as we hurried toward the customer.

"I've showed her every fern in the greenhouse. She found fault with every one. She's got these little bony fingers and she picks everything to death."

I knew who she was talking about. I'd been dealing with this customer for years. A long time ago, someone had dubbed her the Bird Lady because of her twiggy fingers, and the name had stuck. In the interest of good public relations, I used the name on her checks. "Hi, Mrs. Smith. How can I help you?"

"I'm looking for a fern, but this girl can't find anything." She plucked her thin, bony fingers through the lush green fronds, almost like she was flicking bugs. Long, oval, and manicured nails stood out against the plant.

"Well, Mrs. Smith, it looks like she's shown you some pretty ones."

Mrs. Smith glanced down her nose at the pile of cast-off plants. "This one is stringy, this one is too thick, and this one will be pot-bound before summer is out." Her thin fingers kept picking and flicking. Bits of broken fronds rained to the ground.

"I'm going to have to ask you to handle the plants more gently. You're breaking the fronds."

Her eyes shot sparks. "Well, if they are that fragile, maybe I don't need one."

"No, ma'am, it's not that you don't need it; you need to learn to care for it. You can't be rough with ferns if you want them to stay nice."

She gave me a look that would melt an anvil, but I resolved to stay firm. "Now, which basket do you want so we can put the rest back in place?"

She settled on a fern and I carried it to her car, readying myself for the ritual of the "white sheet." I wasn't disappointed.

"Now, check the bottom on that pot. I don't want to see a speck of dirt on it." Her thin lips pursed, and her eyes blazed.

As she opened her trunk, I ran my fingers over the pot bottom and showed her it was clean. The sun shone off the white sheet inside, almost blinding me. "See, I keep a white sheet in here, and I don't want you getting a speck of dirt on it."

Holding the pot up for her second inspection was much easier than holding my tongue. Firm but nice, I reminded myself. "You decide if there's any dirt. I can carry it back to the greenhouse just as easy as I brought it out."

She thought for a minute. "No. No. Don't do that."

I settled the fronds around the pot where they wouldn't be

crushed by the trunk lid and closed it. Satisfied, she got into her car and started the engine.

When I walked back into the greenhouse, Candy was hovering around the door. "How'd you do that? I couldn't get her to take anything."

"You have to be firm."

Next day the old brown car pulled into the parking lot again. Candy crawled under a bench looking for weeds to pull. The Bird Lady came in lugging a terra-cotta strawberry pot. "I need you to plant this. Handle it carefully and don't break it."

"Yes, Mrs. Smith. I know it's expensive and once belonged to your mom. What are we going to plant?" She went through her usual hassle of hunting through every plant in the greenhouse. I knew, and she did too, that she'd wind up purchasing green and white striped spider plants like she had last year and all the years before.

Finally, when she'd ruled out every other choice, she declared, "Well, I guess it's spider plants. I don't know why you don't have something different once in a while."

I potted the spiders into the holes in the jar and patted them in nice and firm.

She smirked her little smile. "Be sure to clean off the dirt. I can't have my sheet stained."

I placed the strawberry pot in a clean cardboard box. "There. Now you won't have to worry."

"But I'll have to throw that box away when I get home."

I loaded her and her pot into the car, tired from the battle of the wills. Maybe I'd seen the last of her this year. Yet somehow, she hadn't been quite as obnoxious as usual, and I wondered if part of her huff and puff was show.

The next spring when Mrs. Smith's little brown car pulled into the parking lot, she got out dragging a walker. She wrapped it around her thin frame and held on tight. I hurried out to her, disturbed by her frailness. Maybe I could find a suitable fern and bring it to her so she wouldn't have to struggle through the displays of pansies and perennials.

She met me with the same surly attitude. "Get my pot out of the trunk." She handed me her keys, and I couldn't help noticing her unkempt nails. I carried the pot to her.

"Now, don't drop it. Keep it until I'm ready to plant it."

"Okay, Mrs. Smith, but it's past the time for frost. You can safely put it outside now. What shall we plant?"

"I can't decide. You hold on to it like I said, and don't let it get broke. And don't let anyone else walk out of here with it. Can you remember that? Mind that you do. You know how I love that pot."

She tried to pull up the old sarcastic tone, but somehow it fell flat. Then her lips trembled and she spat out. "I'm not buying anything today."

Slowly she turned and stumbled back to the car, pushing against the walker. I felt like crying. Something had just happened, and I wasn't sure what.

She cranked up her car and prepared to back out. "I'll be seeing you again," she called from her window.

True to her word she was back a few days later for her fern. Strangely, she accepted the first one I brought to the car without shredding leaves. I asked if she was ready for her pot. "No. Hold on to it and take good care of it. When I want it, I'll ask for it. And not a minute before."

Silently hoping she'd take the darned thing home before it got broke, I bid her farewell.

A few days later the phone rang. I knew her voice as soon as she spoke. "Have you still got my pot?"

"Yes, Mrs. Smith. Are you ready to plant it?"

"No! Just promise you'll take care of it until I ask for it. No matter how long it takes, don't let anybody have it."

I agreed, thinking, how odd. In all the years I'd known her, she'd wanted that pot planted near the same time she bought her fern. I slipped the pot in an out-of-the-way place under the fans, hoping it'd be safe. If the darn thing got broke, I'd never hear the end of it.

A couple of weeks later another regular customer came into the greenhouse. "Do you remember Mrs. Smith? She drove the brown car and lived on the street with me. She's been sick all spring and she passed away a few weeks back. Poor old thing couldn't get along with anybody, not even her kids. They hadn't seen her in years, but they came home to haggle over her stuff."

The words washed over me. I'd known her close to thirty years and hadn't known she had kids.

I thought about the strawberry jar waiting under the fan. "Are the kids in town now?"

"No, they went back out West as soon as they disposed of everything."

Not everything, I thought, as Mrs. Smith's words came back

clear as day: "You know how I love that pot. Take care of it and don't let anybody else have it."

What should I do?

Tears misted my eyes as I made up my mind to fill it with green and white spiders. It could sit on my deck until she asked for it.

# With a Little Luck

*By Robyn Kurth*

There were only a handful of guests left on the dance floor as the wedding DJ played the last few requests of the evening. By that time, my fiancé Greg and I were the last people left at our table, and the guests at the surrounding tables were already extending their final wishes of congratulations to the happy bride and groom. The open doors let in a cool early autumn breeze off of Lake Michigan as couples and single guests trickled out of the historic reception hall at the South Shore Cultural Center on Chicago's lakefront.

As Greg and I prepared to leave, we paused to pick up the wedding favors that had been placed in front of each table setting. The favors were enclosed in small white cardboard boxes imprinted with the names of the bride and groom and their wedding date. I had seen similar favors at other weddings I had attended—usually filled with Jordan almonds or some other confection—so I was a bit surprised to see that the box contained two tulip bulbs.

"What a clever idea," I commented as Greg opened his box. "Too bad we don't have a garden yet." With our own wedding planned for the following summer and house hunting just one of the many things we had on our to-do list, neither one of us owned a patch of land that would be suitable to plant any flowers. Greg was currently subletting an apartment unit, and I had recently moved back in with my parents in the suburbs to save money for the life-changing expenses we were anticipating in the coming year.

Greg looked around and saw at least five other abandoned boxes at the neighboring tables. One by one, he picked up the boxes and piled them in front of us. "It's a shame to let all these tulip bulbs go to waste," he said.

"But where are we going to plant them?" I asked. "Don't we need to get them in the ground within the next few weeks?"

"We'll think of something," Greg assured me, stuffing a few boxes in his jacket pockets and handing the rest to me to squeeze into my purse.

Even though Greg has much more of a green thumb than I do, somehow I ended up with all fourteen tulip bulbs. Without a full color picture of the actual tulips, I had no idea what sort of blooms I could expect in the spring, but I looked forward to finding out. The coming year, after all, was supposed to mark the beginning of a new life for both of us.

Soon after our friends' wedding, I showed the tulip bulbs to my mother as we sat at the kitchen table. "I know that I need to plant these before the ground freezes up," I told her, "but I don't think we're going to have time to go house hunting for another few months."

Mom looked out of the kitchen's bay window at a bare patch of dirt next to her sun deck. "You could plant them out there," she said. "I never got around to planting the impatiens this year."

A few hours later I was kneeling in the dirt with a gardening spade in my hand, carving out fourteen holes in the black earth. As I placed each tulip bulb in its designated spot, I realized that my parents' backyard was the ideal location to plant these special wedding favors; Mom and Dad had recently celebrated their thirtieth wedding anniversary, and I couldn't think of better role models to have as Greg and I prepared for our own marriage.

I carefully spread dirt over the bulbs and watered down the flower bed. I was such a novice at planting flowers that I didn't even think about using fertilizer to ensure that the tulips would appear in the spring. I wasn't even sure if I could successfully get the tulips to bloom for more than one season. But in some way I felt that with a bit of work, a lot of love, and a little luck, everything I was anticipating in the coming year would blossom into something beautiful.

Six months later, the green stems pushed their way out of the earth like sturdy upright soldiers. The tight buds soon blossomed to reveal tulips with creamy white petals and a matching set of tulips that were rosy pink.

The perennials returned for several seasons afterward. When the tulips first bloomed in my parents' garden, Greg and I had recently purchased our first house. The tulips continued to bloom two years later when we were preparing for a cross-country move from Chicago to Orlando; two years after that, I was able to "visit" the tulips in their flower bed when we made the long-distance trip back to Mom and Dad's house to celebrate our son Alex's first birthday.

Just the sight of those upright soldiers in the garden reminded me of how many things could grow with a bit of work, a lot of love, and a little luck.

# Must-Know Info

# The Secret's in the Soil: Preparing and Amending Soil for Ultimate Plant Success

*Cathy Slovensky*

ike most endeavors in life, a good foundation often ensures success, whether you're building a house, creating a business plan, dressing for a red-carpet event—or digging a garden. Most seasoned gardeners will tell you that the key to success in gardening begins with the soil. Even if you're fortunate enough to live in an area of the country that has premium soil (versus living on a dry, rocky riverbed), knowing basic soil nutrition will help you give your plants the best start possible, whether you're growing herbs, flowers, fruits and vegetables, shrubs, or trees.

Plants, just like people, need balanced nutrition in order to perform at their best. They produce their own food through photosynthesis, the process whereby plants use the sun's energy to convert carbon dioxide (carbon and oxygen, or $CO^2$) and water (hydrogen and oxygen, or $H_2O$) into sugars and starches. Plants also need macronutrients, such as nitrogen, calcium, phosphorus, potassium, sulfur, and magnesium; and micronutrients, such as zinc, chloride, molybdenum, boron, iron, copper, and manganese. Water dissolves the nutrients found in soil, which are then available to the plant's root system. If the soil is lacking certain nutrients, or has an over-abundance of others, this can affect the plant's growth.

You can get some idea of what type of soil you have by squeezing a handful of damp soil. Does it hold together or crumble easily? If it crumbles apart too easily, it may contain too much sand. Is the imprint of your hand on the surface of the soil? It may contain too much clay. When you rub the soil together between your thumb and fingers, does it leave a smear or is the texture grainy? Usually a long smear indicates high clay content, while grittiness usually indicates sand.

While these simple observations give you some information about your soil, the best way to determine what your soil contains is through soil testing. Your local Cooperative Extension Agency can help you find links to independent labs that perform this service. Fees range from fifteen to thirty dollars for the home gardener, which is money well spent when you consider that it takes the guesswork out of soil amendment. Besides testing for the nutrients listed above, most labs also test for soil composition (sand, clay, etc.), pH, and contaminants, and give you recommendations for how to improve your soil. Receiving all of this information helps you determine what adjustments to make depending on what you're growing in your garden.

Most of us think of soil as a static composition, but it's actually a dynamic dance, alive with insects, worms, and microorganisms that are eating plant and animal refuse and releasing nutrients back into the soil. Every garden should contain a large amount of organic matter (such as compost, peat moss, rotted manure, etc.). This not only feeds the soil, but it also aerates it, making it easier for root systems to thrive. While you can buy organic matter at garden centers and superstores, an inexpensive alternative is to have your own compost pile. Composting yard and kitchen waste will eventually produce rich, dark humus that can be worked into your garden each year. You can look online or in most gardening books to learn the process. Composting has become au courant these days because of the new revolution in green ideas (Oprah even featured it on a recent show!), but many gardeners have been composting long before it became popular "news."

Knowing your soil's nutritional makeup will also help you fertilize intelligently. Fertilizer can harm as much as it can help if it's applied incorrectly. For instance, while all plants need some nitrogen, lawns need a much larger amount of it than flowering bulbs, perennials, and fruit trees, which need higher amounts of phosphorus. When you see the numbers on a fertilizer bag—such as 10-10-5 or 30-5-10 and so on—the first number is nitrogen content, the second is phosphorus, and the third is potassium. Nitrogen builds healthy leaves (which help the plant manufacture more food), phosphorus stimulates root growth, and potassium helps build strong roots and stems and improves cold-hardiness. So your lawn may need a fertilizer with a ratio of 36-6-6 while your roses need a different ratio, such as 10-10-5. If you use the same fertilizer for your tomatoes that you use for your lawn, you may have beautiful tomato vines—but no fruit. Knowing these ratios help you determine what type of fertilizer to use depending on what you're growing.

While this is an elementary introduction to the importance of soil nutrition, the most important thing to remember is that the quality of your soil will ultimately determine success or failure in your gardening endeavors. You can invest in the healthiest plants on the market, but if you plant them in poor soil, eventually they will not thrive. Even plants such as hollyhocks and coreopsis, which are known for thriving in poor soil, deserve to put their feet into a healthy soil bed. When you prepare your soil and continue to maintain it each year by top-dressing with organic matter and other nutrients, even weeding isn't a chore. Seeing your soil as a living, dynamic composition rather than just plain dirt will encourage you to nurture and feed it, and you will be the one who reaps the biggest benefits.

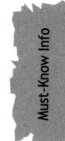

Must-Know Info

Must-Know Info

# Starting Hardy
# Perennials from Seed

*By Suzanne Beetsch*

Sometime ago, when wandering through a plant nursery, I realized that most of the plants I happened to be searching for are just not available commercially. That is when I started in earnest to check into the option of growing plants from seed. I had always grown annual vegetables and flowers from seed; why not perennials?

Perennials are plants that return every year in the garden. They usually increase in size every year and are eventually large enough to divide and transplant or share. Perennials are different from annuals in that they have a protective seed coat that enables the seed to survive for long periods of time if conditions are not exactly ideal for it to germinate in. A perennial seed is still alive even when it is dormant. Deep within the seed is a living embryo that contains all of the information it needs to grow and reproduce.

Most perennial seeds need a cold, moist period (stratification) in order to break down the protective coating on the surface. Germination will take place when the conditions are exactly right for the seed. Some seeds have complex chemical growth inhibitors to prevent germination in vulnerable circumstances, such as a midwinter thaw. This is like a chemical time clock that will send a message to break dormancy and spur germination in the correct season. Chemical growth inhibitors look for a combination of temperature, time, and light to allow the seed to germinate.

Perennial seeds are tough. In nature, they need to survive in temperatures well below freezing in some cases. Most of the seeds I have planted are for Zone 3. I want plants that are sturdy and steadfast, cold-hardy to –20°F, and tolerant of drought, wind, and hot summer sun. These plants include hollyhock, lychnis, penstemons, salvia, verbascum, campanula, clematis, dianthus, and asters.

In nature, plants produce seeds that eventually drop to the ground in the fall to possibly germinate in spring. When you start seed, you basically want to mimic nature as much as possible. Different seeds will have slightly different optimal growing requirements. Some seed, such as Shasta daisies, will require light to germinate and should not be covered with soil. Most will require a light covering of soil.

I order seed from a reputable perennial seed company. Most perennial seed catalogs will list each plant by its botanical name and give you the planting requirements for each one. I like to group my seeds for planting as to whether they need to be exposed to light or if they need a covering of soil. All of the seeds I start require some stratification. This enables me to group my starts all together in one location when I'm finished planting, so I can look in on them over the course of the winter.

When my seeds arrive, I make sure I have plant labels for each plant written in indelible ink. The soil mix I use is a combination of good growing mix, sand, and small gravel. I also have chicken grit on hand, a small one-eighth-inch gravel that is used on the top of pots to keep the seed stable. Some seeds like to be sown directly on top of the chicken grit so that they are exposed to light.

Fill pots with the soil mix. I use four-inch square pots with drainage holes, so that my pots all fit into a planting tray. You can press the soil into the pots with pressure so the soil is evenly distributed and there are no air pockets. I like to soak the pots down with a shower of water before I lay the seed down to make sure all of the soil is stable. Most seed is sown at this point and then covered with a thin layer of soil. You can sow the seed thickly if need be, because you will be transplanting the seedlings in the spring or summer into their individual pots. I cover the sown seed with a thin layer of soil and then a layer of the chicken grit. Make sure the seed is pressed into the soil well and has good contact with it. When all the pots are filled, put them into a tray with drainage holes. I put the tray outdoors (in January) on the north side of the house. Placing the tray on the north side will minimize the variance in temperature during sunny days. On top of my trays I shovel snow and allow the seeds to have their dormant period. If the snow melts off during the winter, I try to keep it covered with snow from other parts of the yard.

Around May, some of the seedlings will have begun to show signs of life. Continue keeping them on the north side and let them emerge slowly. When the seedlings are an inch high, they can be transplanted into individual pots to grow further until they're ready for transplanting to the garden site. The timing varies on individual species.

Planting perennials from seed results in a vast number of plants, so you usually have extra to share with other gardeners. It is a process that takes some patience, but the rewards are fascinating. The varieties to try are endless.

Must-Know Info
# Gardening with Dogs
*Jean M. Fogle*

While dogs enhance our lives in many ways, gardening with them can be quite a challenge. Romping through the beds, pulling up new plants, and digging holes the size of small craters are just a few ways your dog can wreak havoc in the garden. By employing dogwise strategies, you can make sure your best friend doesn't become your garden's worst enemy.

## Fencing

Traditional fencing comes in many different styles to complement your landscape. Picket, wrought iron, or privacy fence is the best way to ensure your dog's safety. While this type of fencing will keep your dog safe at home, it won't protect your landscaped beds. Using the fence as a backdrop, you can add flower beds outside of the yard where flowers will be protected from your canine companion. Since dogs love to run the perimeter of their property, you should leave an eighteen- to twenty-four-inch space inside the yard between your beds and the fence. This allows your dog to patrol for squirrels and other intruders without trampling your plants.

Originally used to keep deer out of landscaped areas, a weather-resistant polypropylene mesh grid fence is now being used to keep dogs at home. For a woody perimeter, this fencing is excellent as it is virtually invisible and blends in with the landscape. Installation is easy to do, since the fence can be attached to existing trees, and the cost is far lower than traditional fencing. The fence can also be installed so it is easily removed when it is not needed.

## Paths

Mulch or stone walks are nice additions to the garden and give you a way to access plants that might be out of reach. Since dogs are creatures of habit, try to place your paths where your dog already runs. If your dog seems interested in a certain area of a new bed, try using large stones to block access.

## Containers

If you have trouble with some tender plants being damaged, try growing them in containers. Lightweight containers are good for moving to different parts of the garden to add color. Heavier containers can be used to discourage trampling in some areas.

## Border Fencing

Border fencing in front of your plants is a good way to keep your dog out of the beds. There are many different styles available, and you can even make your own with supple trimmings such as willow branches. Once your dog has learned not to go into the bed, you can remove the fencing.

## Raised Beds

When adding new beds you might consider raised beds. Besides adding good drainage for the plants, the beds are less accessible to your dog. Stone, brick, or timber can be used to construct the beds.

Gardening with dogs is always entertaining. Their antics will make you laugh, and their ability to live in the moment is infectious. The joy they bring into our lives is well worth the compromises in the garden. By using dog-friendly gardening concepts, you can make sure your pet doesn't become a pest.

## Must-Know Info
# Choosing Low-Maintenance Roses
*Cathy Slovensky*

You might think that "low-maintenance" when applied to roses is a contradiction in terms, with images of black spot, aphid invasion, powdery mildew, anthracnose, and pruning shears coming to mind, but in today's rose market, you can find a disease- and insect-resistant, drought-tolerant, and winter-hardy rose that will bloom summer through fall (and beyond for mild climates). In the past, breeders sometimes sacrificed scent for show, but modern rose breeders are listening to gardeners who want roses that are low-maintenance and fragrant. Now the biggest problem for gardeners is trying to make a decision out of all the wonderful low-maintenance roses available.

How about a cherry red, lightly spicy rose that blooms every five to six weeks until the first hard frost, is disease-resistant, cold-hardy (to Zone 5 and below if protected), self-cleaning (no deadheading), and drought-tolerant? Rose breeder William Radler planted his first rose when he was nine years old; what followed was a lifelong love affair with roses and a goal to "breed the maintenance out of roses." In 2000, his Knock Out Rose, with the qualities described above, won the prestigious All

American Rose Selection (AARS) award.

The original Knock Out Rose, considered a landscape shrub rose, averages three to four feet high and three to four feet wide, has flat-cup blooms (about three to three and a half inches wide), and vigorous mossy green foliage; in the autumn, the foliage turns deep purple and spent blooms form rose hips for winter interest. The second-generation Double Knock Out Rose sports cherry red double blooms and shares all the low-maintenance aspects of the first rose. If you prefer a different color, check out the Pink Knock Out, Pink Double Knock Out, Rainbow Knock Out (an AARS winner in 2007), Blushing Knock Out, and Sunny Knock Out roses. Photos of the Knock Out family can be seen at the Knock Out website (www.theknockoutrose.com), where you can also check on retailers who have them in stock.

If you're looking for a "groundcover" rose, Flower Carpet roses are a good low-maintenance choice. Introduced by Anthony Tesselaar International and developed by German rose breeders Noack Rosen, these disease-resistant, drought-tolerant roses are beautiful planted en masse in colors ranging from red to white and everything in between in both single and double blooms. They vary in height (anywhere from eighteen to twenty-four inches tall) and spread up to forty inches, so they're extremely versatile as a landscape rose. You can view photos of these award-winning roses and read more about their habits at http://www.tesselaar.com/plants/flowercarpetroses/.

And last, but certainly not least, if you want disease resistance, cold-hardiness (some to Zone 3), heady, intoxicating fragrances, every imaginable color and subtle variation (save blue), for any corner of your garden or landscape (shrub, compact, or climbers), Kordes roses meet the criteria. The Kordes family has been hybridizing roses in Germany for more than one hundred years. Wilhelm Kordes III, who took over the family nursery nearly eighteen years ago, has been concentrating on producing pesticide-free, low-maintenance roses, and this is good news for those of us who are concerned about the environment, not to mention one less garden chore.

A favorite Kordes rose for rose growers is 'William Baffin'. Here are just a few of its qualities: it is six to nine feet tall and seven feet wide; has dark pink semi-double blooms and dark green foliage; is deeply fragrant and resistant to black spot, powdery mildew, pests, and disease; is cold-hardy to Zone 3; is loved by butterflies; blooms the first year and is a repeat bloomer; can be used as a cut flower or ornamental or grown in beds, borders, or hedges; and produces large red rose hips in the autumn. What's not to like? You can see photos of Kordes roses at Wayside Garden's website (http://www.waysidegardens.com).

As a final caveat, many roses that are not advertised as such can still be "low-maintenance," so it's good to keep an open mind. For Mother's Day 2004, I received a Bella'roma hybrid tea rose (Jackson and Perkins 2003 Best Rose of the Year) that has exhibited every quality of low-maintenance roses, including surviving the occasional snow in winter and the ninety-degree summers that we experience in eastern Washington. It scores on all levels for what you want in a hybrid tea rose: beautiful color, incredible scent, beautiful foliage, and upright growth habit—and it's disease-resistant. The fragrance from one cut stem permeates an entire room inside, and when we sit outside on our patio, we can smell it from ten feet away, even if just one bud is blooming. Dried petals from Bella evoke a sweet tea scent and still maintain their color even when air-dried. Bella is a rose that has certainly lived up to its name!

If you want to find out what roses are low-maintenance in your area, call your local county extension agent or rose society for suggestions. Here's a short list of a variety of different types, sizes, and colors of many gardeners' favorites in terms of low-maintenance roses: 'Harison's Yellow', 'Mme. Isaac Pereire', 'Linda Campbell', 'Belle de Crécy', 'Queen Elizabeth', 'Fantin-Latour', 'Blanc Double de Coubert', 'Frau Dagmar Hartopp', 'Mermaid', 'Carefree Spirit' (2009 AARS winner, Jackson and Perkins), 'New Dawn', 'Gourmet Popcorn', and 'Sea Foam'. All of these can be found either through your local nursery or garden center or from nurseries online.

## Must-Know Info
# Herb Gardening Tips
*Barbara E. Richardson*

There's something magical about herbs: a little fresh thyme, rosemary, and chives can turn bland potatoes into an encore-worthy side dish, and the fragrance of chamomile tea or a bouquet of lavender has the power to transform your mood. These treats for the senses are never better than when you grow them yourself. Fancy yourself the magician and try it!

Many herbs, such as basil, parsley, dill, and cilantro, require the same conditions as sun-loving annual flowers and vegetables: well-drained, moderately moist, fertile soil with a slightly acid pH (around 6.0) and at least six hours of full sun per day. If such a spot is available right outside your kitchen door, so much the better. If you have limited space, fit herbs into your existing plantings. (If you allow some of your herbs to blossom, they'll attract beneficial insects that prey on garden pests and pollinate vegetable crops.) Herbs also thrive in container gardens, where they can double as ornamentals: imagine a pot of bronze-leaved Thai basil, deep green curly parsley, and variegated golden lemon thyme in an urn on your balcony.

Perennial herbs that originated in the Mediterranean region, including lavender, marjoram, oregano, rosemary, sage, savory, and thyme, require excellent drainage, full sun, and plenty of air circulation to thrive and develop the best flavor. By planting these perennials in pots, you can create ideal soil conditions. In cool regions of the country, this also allows you to easily bring them indoors to overwinter. Gradually acclimate your plants to the lower light and humidity indoors by moving pots to an intermediate location, such as a bright, cool room or porch, for a week or two before introducing them to your home.

As lovely as they are in your teacup and tabbouleh, most mint species can be a challenge in the garden. They grow too well, invading other beds and smothering other plants in their path. If you have enough space in your garden, confine mints to their own bed and install edging around it that extends at least fourteen inches deep and six inches above the soil surface. Or grow your must-haves (who can resist chocolate mint?) in pots or window boxes.

Herb-harvesting techniques vary based on plants' growth habits and needs. For instance, you can literally mow mint to the ground and it will bounce back in two weeks, but you should remove no more than a third of the stems from the Mediterranean herbs so they have enough resources to regrow. Annual herbs like basil and cilantro are best harvested before they blossom. You can cut whole plants, or if you're growing them for their ornamental as well as edible qualities, remove just select leaves and stems.

Some of the best gifts grow in herb gardens. Imagine warming the holiday season or brightening birthdays by sharing your own special blend of chamomile-mint tea, hand-sewn lavender sachets, spicy seasoning mixes, fragrant tarragon vinegar, or rooted cuttings from your rosemary shrub presented in beribboned pots. You may inspire others to join you in your herb gardening magic!

## Must-Know Info
# Hardy Organic Vegetable Gardening
*By Suzanne Beetsch*

Once you have become smitten with the beauty and the fresh, zesty flavors of home-grown vegetables from your backyard garden, you will surely be enticed to plant your garden every single spring. The satisfaction of picking ears of sweet corn, throwing them in boiling water on the stove within minutes, and eating amid butter and salt will surely lead you down the garden path. The advantage of strolling out to the garden to pick your evening salad fixings is a dream come true. There are a myriad of other reasons for planting your own garden as well. Just look at the savings in food transportation costs you will be avoiding. Knowing exactly what goes into your food and where it has been is an automatic green light for garden planning and planting. Organic produce from your own yard will nourish you better than anything you may be able to buy in the supermarket.

Growing a hardy, organic vegetable garden takes some planning. Getting to know the seasons and seasonal temperatures will help the new gardener discover how to follow them and plant accordingly. All you need to get started is a sunny spot (all day sun preferred), some reasonable garden soil, determination, and imagination. These simple things, and the right tools and seed, will make a gardener out of you in only a season or two.

In my Zone 3 garden, I start planning the garden in fall. This is when things have slowed down from the previous garden season, and I can see the ground again because most of the harvesting has been done. Take a good look at the ground you would like to use for the vegetable garden. If it is currently in lawn, you need to remove the grass (via a sod cutter) and get down to the soil, then till or fork the soil. If you have the luck of standing in a previous but dormant garden site, all you need to do is till or fork the soil to prepare it. Loosening the soil will allow you to plant seed and seedlings in it and allow the plants roots to delve deep into the earth for nutrients and water. Good root development in your organic garden plants will create healthy plants.

Organic gardening is the process of growing plants without the use of chemical fertilizers or insecticides. Building up the quality of soil of the particular garden site that you have is a matter of time and materials available. Soil is the basis of successful gardens, and paying close attention to the soil in the planning phase will result in better yields and healthier, happier plants. Scoop up a shovelful of your soil and pick up a handful. Good garden loam should clump together in your hand and then easily break apart as you rub your fingers together. Sandy soil falls on one side of the texture scale and clay is on the other. Your soil should feel somewhere in between. See what is available in your area to add to your soil, should it fall short of perfect.

Fall is a great time for adding amendments to the garden plot. Leaves, compost, peat moss, and so on will help you get started in finding the right balance for your site. Talk to other gardeners in your area to find out how they enhance their organic plots. Adding organic matter to your soil is a must for the gardener. Soil testing is sometimes available through your local Cooperative Extension Agency, and if they don't perform tests, they'll be able to give you information on independent labs that do. Let them know you are starting an organic vegetable garden, and they may have some good local advice as well. I've never had my garden soil tested (I have gardened at my place for fifteen years). I just continue to add compost and leaves to my garden each fall and spring, and the soil fertility continues to be good.

Fall is soil-enhancement time in my garden, but can be done in the spring as well. I am usually anxious in the spring to get planting and would rather have the soil ready. Let's say this is fall, and you have done your soil prep work and you're just going to wait out the winter peering through the seed catalogs. Wait! Fall is the time to plant garlic in my climate. So before you say good night to your prepared garden soil until spring, make some room for garlic. Planting garlic is easy and is a welcome friend come spring. Divide the garlic bulb into cloves. Plant each clove, blunt side down, in a prepared bed or row. Look for good, organic garlic from a local grower at the farmers market or seed catalog. After planting four to five inches apart and covering with soil, mulch with straw or hay, four to five inches deep. Come spring, you will see shoots of garlic coming thru the mulch. Garlic is ready to harvest in late July or August.

Winter is for planning the garden and deciding which seeds to order. Start with thinking seasonally again. Early spring is the time to plant crops that can handle the fluctuating temps and the frosty nights, such as lettuce mixes, beets, onion sets, radishes, kale, peas, and spinach. Order as many of these as you want to get started with. Seed catalogs are a fine way to drift through those January evenings, dreaming of your beautiful, fragrant veggie garden. Next, think of spring planting with broccoli, cauliflower, Swiss chard, carrots, and potatoes. Summer planting (June in my northern garden) is when I set out tomato and pepper plants and put seed in the ground of winter and summer squash, pumpkins, cucumbers, and beans. I like to order seed while thinking of the seasons and what I may do in the garden and when. You can write up a calendar to remind yourself of the seasonal timing. How much seed to order depends on your garden plot size. Figure out which vegetables you want to start with and give yourself enough room to begin with those. Some new gardeners start out with huge gardens while others start with some salad greens and a few herbs. Any size of a garden is a thing of beauty, so just tackle what feels right.

There are a few plants I start indoors instead of planting seed directly into the garden. Those plants are tomatoes and peppers (these are long-season plants and need more growing time than my average ninety days), I also start broccoli and cauliflower and cucumbers indoors. These plant starts can also be purchased at most plant nurseries as well as the tomatoes and peppers. I like starting my own because I can be sure I am growing the varieties that I have selected, and I enjoy doing it. For my northern garden, I start tomatoes and peppers in February, while the broccoli, cauliflower, and cucumbers are started in mid-April. Starting seed is something most people grow into as they garden, because it gives the gardener more varieties and control over growing mediums and fertilizers.

Once spring has arrived—with a chill still in the air—I like to get out into the garden to see if I can work the soil. I like the soil to be somewhat dried out by the wind and sun before I start planting beds. Working in soil that is too wet will compact the earth, which is not ideal for tiny seeds and seedlings. Wait until the earth still feels cool but is not muddy.

When the early spring seeds are in the ground, water if necessary, especially if the ground becomes dry on the surface. Soon the spring and summer crops will be in the ground as well. One can always fill in empty spaces with flowers and herbs to balance out the harvest. Keeping a vegetable garden watered will depend on where you live. I always use mulch in my vegetable garden to decrease the amount of water needed. I use hay or straw, but grass clippings also work. Mulch helps plants' root systems retain moisture, and it helps keep weeds down too, saving time spent weeding. While plants are small seedlings, only a small amount of mulch is needed. As they increase in size, layer on the mulch and keep those roots nice and cool.

Caring for and maintaining an organic vegetable garden is a work of love and effort. Learning to understand the specific needs of plants takes patience. I find that the daily tasks of a garden help me unwind. Harvesting the bounty is an ongoing process throughout the summer. As things become ready to eat, use them in your everyday cooking and base your meals on seasonal foods. You won't believe how delicious your fresh tomatoes with basil

and olive oil are at the end of August! Seasonal planning and eating are what many cultures around the world have done for centuries. It is the way each one of us can truly affect the health of
the planet, by eating local, organic, fresh foods as often as we can.
Growing your own organic vegetable garden will provide you with
a renewed sense of taste and awareness. So start small or start big,
use your garden as an art form, or a place the little ones can dig
for worms. There are as many ways to plant your organic vegetable garden as there are people in this world, so enjoy your own
piece of the earth.

# Tips for Planning a Small Garden: So Many Ideas, So Little Space

*Sarah Chase Shaw*

Small-space planning and design constitutes the ultimate challenge for homeowners and garden designers. It is appealing because it is manageable, simple, and detail-oriented. However, its very simplicity is a challenge. Questions of use should be foremost in the mind of the user: What should I keep? What should I remove? Where should I store the excess? Questions of durability plague the designer: What will it look like in ten years? How will the materials last? Another issue is the changing needs of the users.

A small garden is really an outdoor extension of an indoor environment. Sometimes it is really much more of a furnished room outside than a garden of botanic interest. In all cases, a small garden needs a unifying theme. The design should relate to the architecture of the house, its surroundings, and its interior design. If the space is sheltered, a table and chairs, outdoor lighting, and possibly a water feature are all that is needed to create a pleasant and usable outdoor space.

All gardens are a series of shapes made manifest by plants, hardscape, and often water. Generally, these shapes make reference to the pattern of their surroundings. Determining how your garden will fit into your home and lifestyle is the first big step. From there, your choices become much more concentrated. As with any design project, thorough and up-front planning and design is crucial. A good starting point is to think about how you will use your garden. Make a list of things you will do in your garden, and then measure your space to see how much room you really have. Next, draw your ideas on paper to determine whether your ideas are realistic for your space. Do not overcrowd your space. Like a room in a house, less is more. Ideas and questions to consider include the following:

- **The Site:** Is your site flat? Are the views acceptable? Is the environment noisy? What is the architectural style of your house?
- **The Garden:** Will you be growing vegetables, herbs, and flowers for cutting? Are you growing plants for scientific purposes?
- **The Users:** Do you have small children who need a secure and comfortable place to play? Do you love to cook, dine, and entertain in the out-of-doors? Who will maintain the garden?

Small garden sites are challenging; maintenance is usually the easy part. Capturing the essence of a small space is best achieved through focal points and internal room. This can be accomplished by changing the character of various areas using small terraces, interspersed plantings and paving, a strip of lawn, a water feature, a gravel area, or an herb garden. Organic shapes work well in small gardens to make a space look larger than it is. A meandering path, while short, is a visual journey; a straight path in a small space is not. An indirect path through a small space can be created with simple planting masses placed at intervals to interrupt the route, or with the placement of a central feature, like a fountain or a raised herb garden, around which the visitor must pass.

Planning a garden is similar to decorating and furnishing a house: it cannot be done without knowing what materials and techniques are at your disposal. If you're starting from scratch, the following ideas may be very helpful.

- A small transition step can break the horizon and provide a visual check. A series of steps or large shallow steps, softened by plantings, introduces an immediate sense of direction and structure in the garden.
- Plant choice is very important. Don't choose one of everything. Rather, find a palette that gives you color and texture throughout the growing season. If you are interested in a production garden, analyze your site for best sun exposure. Consider raised beds; they will literally contain the fruits of your labor. Understand in advance the spatial and growing requirements of the crops or flowers that you want to grow.
- Grass is inappropriate for small spaces unless the main objective is to contain small children, or as a path system within a garden.
- Seating, both mobile and immobile, is integral to the garden.

Generally, one permanent seat in a small garden is all that is
needed. When planning a seating area, consider the view,
wind protection, sun exposure, and the surface on which the
seats will be placed.

- Hardscape adds visual and textural interest in a small garden. Brick, stone, tile, and gravel can be mixed to produce a
rich and complex tapestry effect. However, it is important to
pick your materials carefully as competing paving patterns
can result in a visual cacophony in a small space.

- Structure, of the three-dimensional sort, is important for
directing views; creating focal points or an illusion of space;
providing entrances, exits, and corridors; and establishing
boundaries. Well-designed garden structures made of durable
materials involve money, but will never be regretted. They
ensure a sense of enclosure and privacy, as well as a marvelous
background and support for plants. Trellis structures, gates,
vines, and small ornamental trees or shrubs are mechanisms
for providing good year-round structure in a small space.

- A simple water feature can make an attractive focal point or
vista termination. In dry climates, water adds humidity, and
its very sound is a welcome relief during the heat of summer.
Water features are also helpful in masking unwanted envi-
ronmental noise. These elements, however, require a lot of
attention and can be a maintenance problem in areas with
temperature fluctuations.

- Containers and sculptural elements are wonderful additions
to a small garden, as they are great vehicles for instant
changes of mood, effect, and display. Containers made of

stone, lead, and wood, or clay terra-cotta or reconstituted stone are recommended because of their inherent sculptural qualities.

Small-space garden design offers an opportunity to achieve elegant simplicity in design and detail. The combination of color, texture, and three-dimensional organic and inorganic character is an opportunity that no garden designer should let pass.

Must-Know Info
# Inviting Butterflies and Hummers into Your Garden
*Jean M. Fogle*

Butterflies and hummingbirds are creatures of ephemeral beauty. Their short stay in our gardens adds a depth and dimension that flowers alone cannot give. As they flit from one flower to another, they grace us with their beauty and give us a sense of peace. By planting their preferred nectar plants in the proper location, you can be sure they will be regulars to your garden this year.

Since annual flowers bloom all season, be sure to plant plenty of them midspring. Petunias, salvia, lantana, cleome, and nicotiana are annuals that have a big bonus! In addition to being lovely, these plants attract both hummingbirds and butterflies. Locating the plants in sunny areas of the garden that are sheltered from the wind will encourage butterflies to stay and visit for a while. Hummers are attracted to red, so plan to plant plenty of flowers with red blooms. Apparently, bees cannot see the color red, so they don't visit red flowers, leaving the nectar available for the hummers. Mine are known to always check the laundry when a red article is hung out! With their long beaks, tubular flowers are easier for them to feed from. Be sure to limit spraying for insect problems; try to use organic solutions instead. Plant some hummingbird- and butterfly-friendly plants and get ready to enjoy the antics of hummingbirds and the beauty of butterflies!

Try adding some of these annuals, perennials, and climbers to your garden to encourage these flying beauties.

## Hummer Plants

**Bee Balm:** If you need something to spread in an area that blooms most of the summer, bee balm is the perfect plant.

**Bugleweed (Ajuga):** This perennial groundcover has blue blooms, but hummers love it anyway. It is the first plant to bloom when hungry hummers return from the south.

**Cardinal Climber:** An annual climbing plant, Cardinal Climber quickly covers structures and adds a summer of wonderful red flowers.

**Columbine:** Columbine blooms early and is a great plant for any shady garden.

**Coral bells:** This perennial is an early-blooming perennial with tiny flowers that hummers love.

**Fuchsia:** Used in containers and hanging baskets, this annual plant has lovely tubular flowers that hummers love!

**Salvia:** The tubular, fiery red flowers are a great magnet for hummers.

**Trumpet Creeper (also called Trumpet Vine):** A woody climber that is native in many areas, Trumpet Creeper has orange red flowers that attract hummers.

# Butterfly Plants

**Butterfly Bush (Buddleia):** This is a woody shrub that loves sun and blooms all summer long. Many varieties are available in a variety of colors.

**Butterfly Weed:** The orange cluster of flowers of this native wildflower are usually covered with butterflies.

**Cosmos:** Blooming in a variety of colors, this annual is easy to grow and is a favorite of butterflies.

**Lantana:** Another sun-loving annual, lantana's bright flowers are very attractive to butterflies.

**Nicotiana:** An old-fashioned annual, this plant gives a season of color.

**Phlox:** Sweet-smelling flowers of many different colors, phlox is a great perennial for bringing in butterflies.

**Zinnia:** The flat-topped flowers of zinnias give butterflies a great perch for feeding.

## Must-Know Info
# Creating Theme Gardens with Children
*By Linda E. Allen*

A garden—the perfect classroom. In a medium that is hands-on and does not have to be censored, a garden can nurture the innate curiosity and creativity in your child or the adult child in you. It can keep you and your child learning and curious and possibly sow the seeds of a lifelong hobby, interest, or even career. Of course, science is the obvious "course" in the garden, with botany, biology, horticulture, and ecology lessons already prepared. Math, art, literature, and even social studies activities can also be integrated into your gardening "curriculum."

Less expensive than video games, a garden provides you a return on your investment (a lesson in economics!) with the beauty and fragrance of flowers, the harvest of fresh vegetables, and the pride of creating and growing a garden. Family togetherness and serenity are additional, intangible benefits from garden activities.

A child's garden is just that—a place for a child to observe, explore, and interact with nature in its purest form. It doesn't have to be large; in fact, small is good, so that it is not overwhelming or intimidating. As the child and his or her interests grow, the size of the garden can grow also. Child-size garden tools help master the chores in the garden, making them more like fun than work. Even old spoons can be "'borrowed" for small hands to use for digging.

Getting started is simple—a small plot of dirt or potting soil, plastic pots, clean yogurt containers, or even recyclables like old boots and a variety of seeds are the basics; nothing elaborate or expensive. A garden is not for instant gratification; it encourages and teaches patience as we check and double-check to see whether the seed treasures we buried in the soil have peeked out from their hiding places. Fast-sprouting, quick-growing plants are best for younger children to maintain their interest. Sunflowers, radishes, marigolds, lettuce, gourds, beans, and nasturtiums are good for first-time, eager gardeners and are almost fail-proof.

A seed is a promise for the future. From all sizes, like specks of dust barely visible to the unaided eye, to baseball-size coconuts, they hold all the genetic information and nutrients to help fulfill the promise. Just add soil, water, light, and TLC. Tiny seeds can become jumbo, heavyweight tomatoes or huge pumpkins that can grow into the "pumpkings" of the garden.

Garden families that have giant as well as miniature members are fun for children and can teach them the variety and diversity of similar plants. Tomatoes, cucumbers, watermelons, pumpkins, dahlias, and zinnias all have both jumbo and pixie sizes, plus they are easy to grow. Children can practice measuring and weighing pumpkins, watermelons, and tomatoes during their growth cycles, while the prolific zucchini is especially noted for its length. There are many contests for the biggest specimen of these plants where young gardeners can show off the fruits of their labor. At the other extreme are the miniatures: patio or bite-size tomatoes, "baby" basketball-size watermelons, and mini pumpkins that just fit a small hand.

These plants also provide other fun diversions for children in the garden. Some boast nontraditional colors like orange tomatoes and ghostly white or gray pumpkins. Melons, pumpkins, squash, and cucumbers are excellent for "tattoos" or autographs. Just gently scratch your name or a design in the fruit when it is small. As it grows, the "tattoo" or signature will grow and expand with the plant.

The fast-growing sunflower can become a yardstick to compare a child's height with the sunflower's growth. When the sunflower head is just taller than the child, mark his or her height on the stem with a bright ribbon. Watch as the ribbon grows higher and higher as the sunflower eventually towers above the child. Sunflower heads also make interesting autumn decorations and good bird feeders to invite birds to your yard in the autumn and winter.

Every child needs a magical, enchanted place to daydream, imagine, and make believe. A towering teepee of beans, nasturtiums, or any fast-growing, climbing plants provides a perfect child retreat. A simple frame can be made with six bamboo poles or even broomsticks approximately six feet long. Plant the base firmly in the soil in the shape of a "C." The opening will be the door. Tie it together at the top with rope or old nylon hose. Plant beans, nasturtiums, morning glories, or other vining plants at the base of each pole. For an indoor/outdoor "carpet," plant shade-loving grass seed inside the teepee, and you have a shady retreat perfect for picnics, games, tea parties, reading, or even a camouflage fort.

Theme gardens are a fun and popular way to personalize a child's special interest or to highlight similar plants and can serve as a springboard for additional garden activities. Some suggestions are:

**Fairy Garden:** A fairy garden is a magical place to share favorite fairy tales with your favorite child. Create a house for the fairies and pixies that folklore claims frequent the garden in the moonlight. Bury half of a six- or eight-inch clay pot on its side in the ground, tucked in among the flowers for a hiding place for the shy fairies who work their garden magic at night away from curious human eyes. Place a carpet of moss or soft grass inside and furnish with smooth stones and bark. A small pebble path leading to the entrance helps attract fairy guests. Plant creeping plants like ivy to cover the pot or decorate with paint or dried flowers or bark and herbs. It is whispered that fairies are particularly fond of hollyhocks, lamb's ears, forget-me-nots, lavender, thyme, violas and violets, and snapdragons.

**"What Time Is It?" Garden:** Let your garden tell the time during the lazy days of summer. Morning glories greet the day with their bright blossoms early in the morning. Sunflowers follow the sun with their cheery faces all day—the reason they are so named. Four-o'clocks bloom just in time for afternoon tea in the garden, while moonflowers* seem to glow in the evening and have a wonderful fragrance. You may even be able to watch the moonflower unfurl from bud to full blossom in just five to eight minutes. All these plants are easy to grow for a young gardener's

*Moonflowers (datura) are very poisonous if ingested.

success. Be sure to add thyme to your time garden for a fun play on words.

**Animal Garden:** Common names of many plants come from their resemblance or similarities to animals. Create a garden "zoo" with these plants: lamb's ears, as soft and fuzzy as the real animal; cockscomb, like a bright red rooster's comb; elephant ears, the size of Dumbo's ears; snapdragons, with blooms that can be squeezed to look like a miniature dragon's mouth opening and closing. Even the lowly dandelion received its name from the French words dent de lion or lion's tooth, because its jagged leaves resemble the teeth of a lion. Other garden "animals" include mouse-ear, tiger and spider lilies, larkspur, hens and chicks, bee balm, butterfly bush, and zebra plant. There is even a unicorn plant, which might be as difficult to find as the mythical animal.

**"Sense"ational Garden:** "Please touch" could be the sign for this garden of herbs. Involve the senses of taste, touch, and smell with basil, chives, cilantro, sage, parsley, dill, rosemary, thyme, and mint. Herbs offer a variety of textures, tastes, and aromas in the garden and are easy to grow. Many have interesting histories and uses. For tasting experiences in the garden, children should always be supervised. Not all plant parts are safe to eat.

The dynamic, microworld of the garden changes seasonally, daily, and even hourly. Simple activities from the "good old days," like a garden scavenger hunt, fashioning flower dolls from hollyhock blossoms, crafting miniature boats from pea pods, or making seed collages and pressing flowers can encourage creativity while making pleasant memories for the future.

---

## Must-Know Info
# New Job for Old Wheelbarrows
### By Danita Cahill

---

I like imaginative, recycled planters to set around in my flower beds. Old, worn-out wheelbarrows are one of my favorites, since they blend in well with our country setting and lend a whimsical touch to the garden.

I look for well-used wheelbarrows at garage and estate sales, where I'll pay up to five dollars apiece. After hauling my new, often rusty treasures home, I drill drainage holes in the bottoms. If rust has already eaten some holes through the tubs, fine with me, I can skip this step. Next, I fill the wheelbarrows with a quality potting mix and swirl in a handful of slow-release fertilizer—two handfuls if it's a large wheelbarrow.

Then comes the fun part—a trip to a garden center or nursery to pick out plants. Trees cover most of our property with shade, so I choose annuals and perennials that thrive in sun-dappled light. A few of my favorites for partly sunny to shady plants to grow in a wheelbarrow are pansies and violas, campanula (bell-flowers), impatiens and 'New Guinea' impatiens, fuchsias, dianthus (carnation family), tuberous and wax begonias, hardy geraniums (cranesbills), hostas, and coleus.

But be bold. Discover your own favorites. Just follow this one simple rule: Choose plants with similar light and watering requirements for each wheelbarrow you fill. This information is usually printed on the growing tags. No tag? No problem. Just ask one of the nursery staff to help clue you in.

When it comes to container plantings, my motto is, "The more the merrier," and filling a wheelbarrow is no different. The more flowering plants I can squeeze in, the better the show. I group plants especially thick at the deep end of the tub, where they have extra room to spread their roots. The tallest flowers I settle toward the middle. I plant trailing or vining plants that can withstand partial sun, such as alyssum, lobelia, fuchsia, creeping fig, Lamium, or Swedish ivy around the edges to spill over the sides.

If you have a mostly sunny yard or garden, don't despair—recycled wheelbarrows will still work for you. Just choose plants that prefer full sun. And plan to water more often than if the wheelbarrows stayed in the shade—probably every day during scorching weather.

I enjoy my old wheelbarrows. I think they make cheap, interesting, and green planters. And if I want to relocate them, it's a breeze to wheel them to another spot in the garden.

Must-Know Info

# Designing Your Landscape

*By Larissa Hise Henoch*

Your landscape speaks volumes about who you are and gives you the ultimate chance to be creative. There are a few things outside personal taste to keep in mind when designing your landscape, however. Find out what zone you live in by checking the climate zone map on page 234. You will want to plan to us only those plants that are hardy to your zone. Browse through your local nursery to see the selection of plants your area has to offer before purchasing. When you begin laying out your plans, you'll have a better idea of what's available to you. Also, consider the amount of sun the different parts of your property gets and the direction of prevailing winds, as some plants will do best in protected areas.

In many cases, the front yard is purely decorative and serves as a welcome mat for your guests. It should look vibrant, healthy, and inviting throughout the changing seasons. Your personal taste will obviously play a big role in the choices you make, but keep in mind that the most beautiful landscapes frame the house and accentuate the positives and camouflage the negatives. Establish your backdrop with trees and shrubs of various shapes and textures. Then, enhance the backdrop with colorful perennials and/or annuals to highlight your house. Carefully consider your color scheme. You may want to use complimentary colors such as blue and orange, yellow and purple, or red and green, or analogous colors such as blue, purple, and pink; or yellow, orange, and red. Keep in mind that different colors will give your landscape different effects. For example, warm colors such as red and orange are visible from a distance, cool colors such as blue and violet help give an open feeling to small spaces, white flowers highlight gardens at night, and gray-green foliage helps blend various colors.

While the front yard usually serves as the showcase of your property, the backyard is a place where family and friends gather together to relax and have fun. To make your backyard more inviting, consider a patio, deck, fence, or outdoor dining area, then enhance these areas with your landscape choices.

If you plan well, plants can serve as area dividers or privacy screens, and a well-planned arbor will provide you and your guests with a comforting shelter. You will want uninterrupted movement in your backyard, so avoid sectioning it off too much. Evergreen hedges make the best year-round privacy screens and camouflage unsightly areas or neighbors' yards. However, evergreens are slower growing than many deciduous hedges, so this is something you may want to keep in mind.

When planning your landscape, pay close attention to the amount of sun, shade, and wind your backyard gets throughout the seasons to create a comfortable outdoor living space year round. You will want shady areas as well as areas of full sun so you can have the best of both worlds. And if you live in a very windy area, you may want to make landscape choices that will give you some relief by selected hardy plants that can acts as a windscreen.

While paths and walkways serve as a transition for one area to another, they can also add texture and color to your landscape. Consider brick, tile, or stone for added interest. If you are building a path from scratch, keep in mind that it should be a minimum of 3½ feet wide, which allows two people to walk comfortably side by side. A curved or winding walkway adds the illusion of a longer distance, whereas a straight walkway visually shortens it.

You might want to add height and dimension with a gazebo, create an outdoor living room with an arbor, or screen off areas with a trellis. Raised beds, which add height, can soften the architectural lines of your house and/or add an interesting design element to separate your garden spaces. They can also improve drainage. You can choose from a variety of textures and colors for your raised beds such as such as redwood, railroad ties, faux wood, brick stone, or mortar. Water features, such as a fish pond or fountain, can add a calming, cooling effect to your garden. Statues and large stones can add an additional point of interest. (Be sure to check with your local authorities as some of these items may be considered permanent structures and could require permitting.)

Whether in the front yard or backyard, trees are a point of focus around which everything else will spring up. There are seven different basic tree forms to consider:

1. Rounded (Maple)
2. Weeping (Willow)

3. Vase Shaped (Elm)

4. Spreading (Oak)

5. Columnar (Cyprus; evergreen) (Poplar; deciduous)

6. Pyramidal (Fir)

7. Conical (Spruce)

Tall evergreen trees frame and create strong vertical lines, while rounded deciduous trees can provide shade to your outdoor living space. When choosing your trees, always consider the amount of space a given tree will need when it is fully grown. This will help you avoid plumbing problems, roof damage, and, in the event you have a fireplace, potential fire hazards.

Shrubs establish shape, line, texture, and color. There are three different categories of shrubs:

1. Deciduous shrubs (such as dogwood, hydrangea, lilac, honeysuckle, and forsythia).

2. Broad-leaf evergreens (such as laurel, rhododendron, magnolia, boxwood, and holly).

3. Needle-leaf evergreens (such as juniper, fir, cypress, spruce, and hemlocks).

There are many annuals (seasonal plants) and perennials (year-round plants) to choose from, depending on your preferences. In all cases, annuals and perennials add interest to a landscape. Annuals such as marigolds, petunias, coleus, geraniums, larkspur, and salvia will provide your landscape with vibrant seasonal colors. (Be sure to keep the seeds for the following year.) Perennials reappear year after year, and in some cases, they can be divided and replanted elsewhere, providing you with more plants over the years. Baby's breath, plumbago, daylilies, iris, and peony are just a few examples of perennials.

Ornamental grasses such as reed grass, pennisetum, and pampas grass add height to your garden, while ground covers such as pachysandras, wild ginger, lily of the valley, ivy, and liriope are great for adding texture under trees and around shrubs. When affixed to a trellis or other tall structure, vines also add height with interest to your landscape. There are a variety of vines available, such as Carolina jasmine, honeysuckle, Boston ivy, and wisteria.

Clearly there are a wide variety of trees, plants, shrubs, vines, and grasses to choose from. Once again, research your area carefully to find out which choices are the best for your location. Once your research is complete, you are ready to begin planning.

Plan your design on paper before you break out the shovel and wheelbarrow. Consider which projects you are going to do yourself and which need to be hired out. Permanent structures should be done in advance of planting your trees and shrubs to avoid potential damage to your new investments. Plan your project in phases, so you don't end up trying to do too much of it at one time. Here are some tips:

1. Make an aerial drawing of your property using graph paper with each square equaling one foot, as shown on Figure 1 on page 231. Use the survey of your property or measure it yourself. Be sure to include any existing trees or shrubs you plan to keep. Mark north, south, east, and west and consider the

amount of daylight a given area gets, as well as the amount of
wind, and how those are affected by changes in the seasons.

FIGURE 1

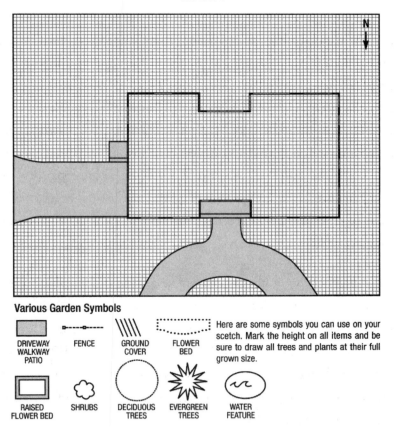

**Various Garden Symbols**

DRIVEWAY
WALKWAY
PATIO

FENCE

GROUND
COVER

FLOWER
BED

Here are some symbols you can use on your
scetch. Mark the height on all items and be
sure to draw all trees and plants at their full
grown size.

RAISED
FLOWER BED

SHRUBS

DECIDUOUS
TREES

EVERGREEN
TREES

WATER
FEATURE

2. Indicate the different terrain of your property as shown in
   Figure 2 on page 232. It is important to choose the correct
   plants for steep terrain. Consult your local nursery for the
   best choices for your zone.

3. Lay a piece of tracing paper over your property layout and sketch the plants you want to use, being sure to allow for their mature size. Consider how a tree or shrub will look from different angles, seasons, and during different times of the day. Try several different designs until you discover the perfect one.

4. A string, rope, or an old garden hose works well to layout the shape of your new gardens. Once you have the rope in position, use biodegradable spray paint to draw your design on your yard. (Remember, if your design requires any walkways, decks, or a patio, it should be completed before you install your new plants.)

5. Remove any unwanted trees, shrubs, and or plants. If you are planning on moving anything to a new location, be sure to protect the root system from the sun and elements.

FIGURE 2

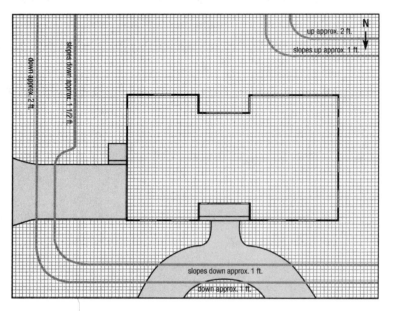

6. Remove unwanted sod, stones, and roots.

7. Turn your soil, adding topsoil, sand, peat moss, and compost as needed.

8. Purchase your new trees, shrubs, and plants, and place them to reflect your design.

9. Take a walk around your property to be sure you approve of your selection.

10. Plant the largest trees or shrubs first. Consult your local nursery for proper installation. Continue planting smaller trees and shrubs.

11. Plant your perennials and annuals.

12. After firmly packing down the soil, water all trees, shrubs, and plants thoroughly to eliminate any air pockets.

13. If you have chosen to use mulch or ornamental stones in your gardens, now is the time to place them. Be sure not to overmulch or place too much stone too close to the base of your plants. (The distance varies by type of plant.)

Congratulations! When you're all done, sit back and enjoy your new landscape. You deserve it!

CLIMATE ZONE MAP

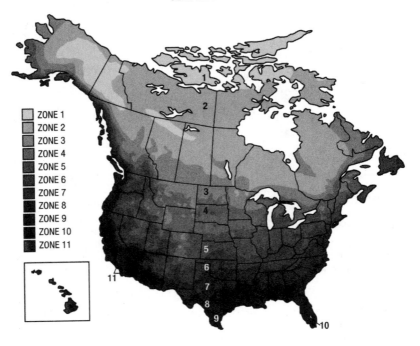

# The Writers

**Linda E. Allen** is the author of numerous magazine articles, essays, and books. *Decking the Halls: The Folklore and Traditions of Christmas Plants* was a finalist for the 2001 Benjamin Franklin Award for history. *Menagerie at the Manger* was named the 2007 Book of the Season by the Book Bank Foundation. Visit Linda's website at http://lindaeallen.squarespace.com.

**Barbara Blossom Ashmun** is the author of *Married to My Garden and Garden Retreats: Creating an Outdoor Sanctuary*. Her garden column appears weekly in the *Portland Tribune*, and she writes for *Fine Gardening* and *Better Homes and Gardens*. Thousands of visitors have enjoyed her two-thirds of an acre garden since 1986.

**Nancy Baker** resides in College Station, Texas, with her husband and golden retriever. Although an author at heart, she began writing in earnest upon her retirement and has been published in numerous anthologies and national magazines. One of her favorite hobbies is gardening, which has provided many good memories.

**Maureen Helms Blake** lives in Spearfish, South Dakota, and is enjoying unofficial early retirement after decades of full-time parenting and homeschooling three children. Currently she is exploring, through the arts, both written and unwritten methods of capturing and communicating ideas. She can be reached at maureenab@yahoo.com.

**Danita Cahill** is a freelance writer, photographer, and master gardener. She lives with her husband and children in a rural neighborhood in the Pacific Northwest, where she still grows pumpkins and tries to remember the sugar when baking pies. You can reach Danita through her website at www.danitacahill.com.

Poet and anthologist **Sally Clark** lives in Fredericksburg, Texas. Her stories and poems have appeared in numerous anthologies for adults and children. She is not much of a gardener, but she does supervise her husband and her son's work from the rocking chair on her shaded porch.

**Jennifer Lynn Clay**, nineteen, has been published almost eighty times in national and international magazines and in several worldwide-syndicated books including *House Blessings* and *Forever in Love*. Her *Chicken Soup for the Soul* publications include *A Tribute to Moms, Preteen Soul 2, Girl's Soul, Teens Talk Middle School*, and *Teens Talk High School*.

**Christine E. Collier** is married with three children and five grandchildren and the author of seven books, including a mystery series and two children's books. Most recently three of her stories have been included in anthologies, including *Guideposts* and a book of childhood Christmas memories published by Adams Media.

**Harriet Cooper** is a Toronto writer who waters her garden under her neighbor's watchful eye. When not tending her garden, she writes personal essays and creative nonfiction for magazines, websites, and anthologies. She also writes articles on health, nutrition, and the environment for magazines and websites.

**Cookie Curci** was born and raised in San Jose, California, where she lives with her family and little dog, Zuzu. She has a bounty of stories and memories inspired by her creative mom and her close-knit family. Cookie has recorded these memories for the next generation to learn from and to enjoy.

**Michele Ivy Davis** is a freelance writer whose stories and articles have appeared in a variety of magazines and anthologies, as well as in newspapers and law enforcement publications. Her young adult novel, *Evangeline Brown and the Cadillac Motel*, was published by Dutton (Penguin Group USA) and has won national and international awards. Learn more at www.MicheleIvyDavis.com.

**Suzan Davis** is the author of *Babes on Blades: Drop Physical, Mental and Spiritual Flab Thru Inline Skating*, and contributor to *Chicken Soup to Inspire a Woman's Soul*, *Chicken Soup for the Dieter's Soul*, and *Chicken Soup's Healthy Living* series. Suzan, Dennis, Katelyn, Savannah, and Little Bear live near Indianapolis and are tormented regularly by Phabulous Phil, Fabulous Fran, and Miss Kitty next door.

**Lola Di Giulio De Maci** is a contributor to several Chicken Soup for the Soul books, including *Chicken Soup for the Teacher's Soul* and *Chicken Soup for the Soul: A Tribute to Moms*. She gathers inspiration for her children's stories, which have appeared in the *Los Angeles Times* and other publications, from her now-grown children and the many children she has taught over the years. Lola has a master of arts in education and English and continues writing from her sunny loft overlooking the San Bernardino Mountains. E-mail: LDeMaci@aol.com.

**Marilyn K. Eudaly** has been published in *Chicken Soup for the Dieter's Soul* and is a member of American Christian Fiction Writers, DFW Ready Writers, Lena Nelson Dooley's critique group, Romance Writers of America, and the Faith, Hope and Love chapter. She lives in Texas with her husband of forty-two years.

**Janice A. Farringer** is a poet and writer living in Chapel Hill, North Carolina.

**Nancy Gibbs** is the author of seven full-length books. For the past ten years Nancy has written a weekly newspaper column for the *Cordele Dispatch*. Nancy has contributed to more than one hundred anthologies, including the *Chicken Soup for the Soul* books, *Guideposts* books, *Stories for the Heart*, *God's Way*, and *God Allows U-Turns*. She also writes for numerous national magazines. She has contributed to *Guideposts*, *Decision*, *Happiness*, *Mature Living*, *On Mission*, *Family Circle*, *Woman's World*, and the *Focus on the Family* newsletter.

**Jean Matthew Hall** is a freelance writer. She and her husband, Jerry, live in Indian Trail, North Carolina. She blogs her "Conversations with God" at http://www.jean

matthewhall.blogspot.com and "Encouraging Words for Writers" at http://wwwjean matthewhallwords.blogspot.com. She is also on the staff of the Write2Ignite Writers Conference (http://www.write2ignite.com).

**Juliana Harris** is an actress/writer/singer whose work has appeared in the *New York Times*, the *Kansas City Star*, the *Mid-America Poetry Review*, and the *Best Times* among others. She lives in Connecticut where she is working on her second novel.

**Roberta Beach Jacobson** (aka the Cat Lady) is an American humorist and author. In 1974, she left suburban Chicago to explore Europe. For all of these years, she's been wandering around, map in hand, scratching her head. Can someone out there please give her directions? She makes her home in a mountainous village on a tiny Greek island. It's the sort of remote spot where animals outnumber people, although some of the animals weren't actually invited. Read her blog at http://blog.seattlepi.nwsource.com/catlady/.

**Jo Rae Johnson** digs dirt. In addition to decorating her yard, Jo Rae enjoys tennis, tea, and text messaging her children. Jo Rae's stories have been included in the *The One Year Life Verse Devotional*, *Chicken Soup for the Soul Kids in the Kitchen*, and *Chicken Soup for the Tea Lover's Soul*, as well as the *Upper Room*. She can be reached at t4me@bellsouth.net.

**Nancy Edwards Johnson** writes stories and memoirs of growing up in the Blue Ridge Mountains of Virginia. She writes plant-related articles as well. Nancy is a past winner of the Sherwood Anderson Short Story Competition and is currently working on a novel and a series of short stories featuring mountain folklore. Nancy has been published in previous "Ultimate" books and has been a longtime contributor to area magazines. She writes a monthly column "Fancy That" for *Latitude Magazine*, Winston-Salem, North Carolina. Her e-mail address is nancyedwardsjohnson@yahoo.com.

**Robyn Kurth** is a freelance writer with more than fifteen years of professional writing experience, with a specialty in "writing for the ear." A native of the Chicago area, she currently resides in Orlando, Florida, with her husband, Greg, and children, Alex and Zell. Ms. Kurth's essays have been published in *Chicken Soup for the Chocolate Lover's Soul* and *Chicken Soup for the Democrat's Soul*. She can be reached at rwordworks@earth link.net.

**Veronica Cullinan Lake** is a retired teacher with a home in New York City and on the Jersey Shore. She writes and paints watercolors, and her free time is spent working in her garden, reading, attending foreign films, walking the boardwalk, and gazing out at the ocean.

Best-selling author **Loree Lough** has fifty-nine short stories, more than twenty-five hundred articles, and sixty-seven award-winning books in print, including *Love Finds You in Paradise, PA*. Visit her website (http://www.loreelough.com) for a chance to win a free copy!

**Christy Lowman** is a freelance writer living in the beautiful foothills of the Great Smoky Mountains in North Carolina. She's had three stories published with *Guideposts* in their Miracle series. She's married to her high school sweetheart, with whom she has a wonderful three-year-old son and another one on the way.

**Anita Machek** writes creative nonfiction and mainstream and historical fiction from her home in DeRidder, Louisiana. Pelican published 6:36, her submission to the Louisiana in Words project, an anthology of short pieces relating one minute in Louisiana. Her story "Come for Tea" appears in *Chicken Soup for the Tea Lover's Soul.*

**Melanie L. McCree** recently won second place in the genre fiction category of the *Writer's Digest* annual short story competition. The author of several short stories and some humorous nonfiction, Melanie hopes to write full-time one day, which would be a dream come true. It would also leave more time for gardening.

**Michelle Close Mills's** work has appeared in *Chicken Soup for the Soul, Pocket Prayers* (Chronicle Books), *The Rocking Chair Reader: Family Gatherings* (Adams Media), and *To Have and To Hold: Prayers, Poems, and Blessings for Newlyweds* (Time Warner's Center Street Books). Michelle resides in Indiana.

**Linda O'Connell's** essays, poetry, prose, and articles have been published in numerous periodicals, anthologies, literary magazines, and newspapers. She and her husband, Bill, enjoy gardening and spending time with their nine grandchildren. Linda is happiest when walking on a beach. She has been an early childhood educator in St. Louis, Missouri, for three decades. E-mail her at billin7@juno.com.

**Linda Kaullen Perkins** has had short stories, articles, and essays appear in *Chicken Soup for the Chocolate Lover's Soul, Chicken Soup for the Soul Kids in the Kitchen, Country Woman Magazine, Woman's World* magazine, and various other publications. Check out her website, www.lindaperkins.com.

**Shirley Dunn Perry** is a registered nurse, workshop leader, writer, poet, author, and publisher of *Ten Five-Minute Miracles: How to Relax.* She teaches poetry and writing as a way of healing in the community. Her work has appeared in, among others, *ByLine Magazine,* the *Write Word, Erete's Bloom, Mutant Mule Review,* the *Laughing Dog, A Gathering of Grandmothers,* and *Brush the Mind Gently.* Biscuit making, hiking, world travel, and watercolors add zest to her writing adventures.

**Felice Prager** is a freelance writer from Scottsdale, Arizona, with credits in local, national, and international publications. In addition to writing, she also works with adults and children with moderate to severe learning disabilities as a multisensory educational therapist. For a sampling of her essays, please visit her website at http://www.writefunny.com or her blog at http://www.writefunny.blogspot.com.

**Lisa Scott** is a writer and voice artist who is most likely to be found in her garden with her two children. Learn more at wivb.com and ReadLisaScott.com.

**Cathy Slovensky** has a B.A. in English literature from Montana State University and is certified in both beginning and advanced master gardening. She is a freelance editor who has published articles on aromatherapy, rodeo, religion, and Montana history, among other subjects. She lives in Walla Walla, Washington, with her husband, Bill, cairn terrier, Tilly, and canary, Rico, and makes frequent trips to Montana to see her children, grandchildren, friends, and family. You may e-mail her at cathy.slovensky.56 @gmail.com.

**Joyce Stark** lives in northeast Scotland. Now retired from the local government, she spends her time writing and traveling. She has written a book on her travels in the areas of the United States that are lesser known in Europe and many stories about her home, family, and friends.

**Susan Sundwall** is a freelance writer, pretty good gardener, and a lover of all things that bloom.

**Annmarie B. Tait** resides in Conshohocken, Pennsylvania, with her husband, Joe, and Sammy the Wonder Yorkie. In addition to writing stories about her large Irish Catholic family and the memories they made, Annmarie also enjoys singing and recording Irish and American folk songs. Contact Annmarie at irishbloom@aol.com.

**Janie Dempsey Watts** writes both fiction and nonfiction. Her essays have appeared in several *Chicken Soup for the Soul* books, *Georgia Backroads*, and in the *Christian Science Monitor*. She lives in Woodstation, Georgia, where she is a successful backyard gardener with her okra, tomatoes, and basil plants.

**Bobbe White** is a professional speaker, banker, and author. She helps organizations that want to find more joy, less stress, and a little balance in their lives using humor and laughter. She is the author of *Life in the Laugh Lane* and coauthor of *Chicken Soup for the Wine Lover's Soul*.

**Ferida Wolff** is the author seventeen books for children and two books of essays for adults. Her work appears in newspapers and magazines, the Chicken Soup for the Soul books and HCI's Ultimate series. She is also online at www.grandparents.com and a columnist for www.seniorwomen.com. Her website is www.feridawolff.com.

# The Must-Know Experts

**Linda Allen** is the author of numerous magazine articles, essays, and books. *Decking the Halls: The Folklore and Traditions of Christmas Plants* was a finalist for the 2001 Benjamin Franklin Award for history. *Menagerie at the Manger* was named the 2007 Book of the Season by the Book Bank Foundation. Visit Linda's website at http://lindaeallen.squarespace.com.

**Suzanne Beetsch** received her degree in holistic health from St. Catherine University in Minnesota. She has been gardening most of her life, working in numerous parks, estates, farms, and nurseries. She now owns a massage therapy business in Bozeman, Montana and lives with her husband and daughter in Belgrade, Montana.

**Danita Cahill** is a master gardener. She is also a freelance writer and photographer. Danita has worked on assignment for newspapers and magazines for the past ten years, writing and photographing human-interest pieces and home and garden features. Prior to that, she owned and operated a retail nursery business and wrote a weekly garden column. You can reach Danita through her website at www.danitacahill.com.

**Jean Fogle** is a co-owner of Fort Valley Nursery (http://fortvalleynursery.com) in Woodstock, Virginia. She is a freelance writer and photographer specializing in garden and horticulture topics. You can visit her website at http://jeanmfogle.com.

**Larissa Hise Henoch** is the art director of HCI Books. Her artistic flair shines through in every landscape she creates. Her passion for gardening began as a toddler working alongside her mother in the yard.

**Barbara E. Richardson** is a lifelong organic gardener with a passion for nature and plants. She holds a BS in plant & soil science from UVM and has helped thousands of gardeners with their gardening questions via her work at the National Gardening Association and Gardener's Supply Company.

**Sarah Chase Shaw** is a landscape architect and freelance writer. She received her bachelor of arts degree from Smith College and a master of landscape architecture degree from Cornell University. Sarah has lived–and gardened–in Flagstaff, Arizona, and Santa Fe, New Mexico. She currently resides in Aspen, Colorado. She is the author of *New Gardens for the American West: Residential Landscapes of Design Workshop*.

**Cathy Slovensky** has a BA in English literature from Montana State University and is certified in both beginning and advanced master gardening. She is a freelance editor who has published articles on aromatherapy, rodeo, religion, and Montana history, among other subjects. She lives in Walla Walla, Washington, with her husband, Bill, cairn terrier, Tilly, and canary, Rico, and makes frequent trips to Montana to see her children, grandchildren, friends, and family. You may e-mail her at cathy.slovensky.56@gmail.com.

# The Photographers

**Sabrina Abercromby's** passion for all things green and flowering began many years ago during a college horticulture class. Now she frequently covers gardening topics as a freelance writer. Her photography has appeared with her articles and on the covers of gardening magazines. She lives in Southern California with her husband Keith.

**Kent Akselsen** (www.Akselsen.com) has photographed a variety of subjects including people, purebred dogs, small animals and nature for many years. His photographs have appeared in a variety of books, magazines, and calendars.

**Kelly Andrews** is a self-taught, freelance photographer. Some of Kelly's favorite subjects include the Jersey Shore, barns, rural scenes, gardens, flowers and wildlife—especially birds. An avid gardener, Kelly plans her gardens carefully to attract birds, butterflies and other garden bugs to supply readily available subjects. She has created several garden areas in her yard including a sunflower garden, shade garden, and various perennial gardens with a goal of providing year-long visual interest as well as food for the birds. Kelly's photos have appeared regularly in magazines, books, posters and calendars. Her fine art prints are available in several New Jersey galleries and many of her images can also be seen on her website, www.thrukellyseyes.com.

**Mary Axiotis** is an amateur photographer who enjoys taking pictures of flowers and the country side, family and friends. Mary started with an Olympus Camedia and now uses a Nikon D60 camera with zoom and macro lens.

**Sarah Hart Boyd** lives in the heart of apple and wine country on the shores of Lake Chelan, Washington. With the help of her husband, Casey, and two young children, they've created a lovely garden among the apple trees in their family's orchard that grows bigger and better every year. Sarah is a self-taught fine artist, who with the inspiration of children, nature and surrounded by a beautiful place in which to live, has developed a passion for photography.

**Kelly Marie Cheek** was born on Lakenheath Air Force Base, England, and moved to the United States in 1994. After graduating from Plantation High School, Sunrise, Florida, she joined the United States Air Force and was stationed at Offutt Air Force Base, Nebraska. Currently she is attending school to be a Early Childhood teacher and spends her down time with her creative writing, amateur photography, and family.

**Sandra C. Covey** is a freelance photographer based in Morton Grove, Illinois. She specializes in photojournalism, portraits, sports, landscapes, music, and entertainment. Sandra possesses a unique eye for composition in landscape photography. Her images from sites in the United States, Mexico, Europe, and Africa make you feel as if you were there. She is a member of the American Society of Picture Professionals (ASPP).

**Jennifer Crites** is a Honolulu-based photographer and writer whose words and images exploring travel, contemporary lifestyles, food, education, and science have been published in magazines and books worldwide. She invites readers to visit her website at http://www.jennifercritesphotography.com.

**Clair Dunn** is a stock and fine art photographer in Vermont, specializing in rural, agricultural, and black and white photography. Enjoy more of Clair's work at www.clairdunn.com.

There's a little known secret about **Sharon P. Fibelkorn**. While known for her keen eye and refined editorial work, she is also an avid gardener. After relocating to the Southwest, she became smitten with the native, drought tolerant plants. The beginning of wildflower season is one of the great joys of her year and she happily waits for those first cheery orange blossoms to greet her in her garden. The native plants of the Southwest continue to amaze and enhance Fibelkorn's personal garden, photographic works, and her life.

**Susan Friedman** (photographer/filmmaker) is an award-winning documentary filmmaker and photographer with twenty-four years of experience in the field of education. She is currently on the faculty at the University of California, Santa Cruz. Friedman has been a still photographer for many years and has had one-women shows both nationally and internationally, including Tokyo, Amsterdam, Berlin, and San Francisco. Her book of documentary photographs for the Sierra Club, *A Separate Place*, was published in 1974. Her work is collected in the Museum of Modern Art in New York, the Oakland Museum, and the Bibliotheque National in Paris. Information about her recent limited edition book *Equus* can be found at: www.susanfriedmanphoto.com. In 2007 Friedman had three major shows of her new work *Equus* with horses, at the San Francisco Museum of Modern Art (MOMA) Café Museo, Spur Gallery in Portola Valley, and SF MOMA Artist's Gallery. Susan can be reached at whatisup@earthlink.net.

**Leslie Goldman**, AKA Your Enchanted Gardener, plants seeds of success for super ripe people and their dreams. *The Ultimate Gardener*, morphed from a "Seed Dream" between Leslie and the publisher, Peter Vegso, at the 2008 Book Expo America. Leslie's companion is Keep the Beet Media Star, the world's first talking beet plant. Keep the Beet's message is that we can each grow our own food, starting with growing a local, organic beet in a pot. "Keep the beet. Eat the beet greens," is Beet's motto. Leslie writes daily on the "Plant Your Dream" blog, and uses photography as a way to show others how he sees the world. You can learn more about Leslie's Enchanted Garden Projects by visiting www.curezone.com/blogs/f.asp?f=92. Posts include; *"Plant Your Dream," "Words Men Need to Know and Women Want to Hear," "The Seven Love Cures," "Job's Tears Grow a Necklace," "Super Ripe Images"* and *"Beet Keepers."*

**Ryan Hutchinson** is an amateur photographer from Halifax, Nova Scotia, Canada. Ryan's main interests in photography lie in wildlife, motorsports, and waterfalls. He is always working to improve his photographic skills. Ryan's photography can be enjoyed at http://www.Ryan-Hutchinson.com

**Maggie Swanson**, a freelance illustrator of over one hundred children's books, lives in Connecticut with her husband, Rick, and two exceptional cats, Tommie and Gracie. She has a woodland shade garden which provides inspiration and subject matter for her watercolors. You can enjoy her work at www.maggieswanson.com.

**Lynn Tait** is a widely published poet and amateur photographer from Sarnia, Ontario, Canada. She began by taking photos while traveling on the back of her husband's motorcycle. Her photos have made the cover of two books: *Sounding the Seconds* and *Ghosts of Water Street* and a cover of *Toward the Light Journal of Reflective Word & Image*. You can e-mail Lynn at lyta@sympatico.ca.

# About the Author

harlie Nardozzi acquired his love for growing plants growing up around his grandfather's farm in Connecticut. When it came time to go to college Charlie decided to attend the University of Vermont so he could major in horticulture. After graduation, he joined the Peace Corps and was assigned to Thailand. There he learned and then taught new agricultural techniques as well as to experiment with different varieties of local crops. These experiences motivated Charlie to go back to the University of Vermont to get a master's in education.

Charlie's Peace Corps experience and his education opened up doors for him at the National Gardening Association. He's worked there on and off since 1988 and is currently their senior horticulturist and spokesperson.

On the side, Charlie keeps himself busy with a variety of different gardening-related projects. He is the author of *Vegetable Gardening for Dummies* and contributed work to *Gardening for Dummies*. He's also contributed to *Keeping a Garden* and other *Better Homes and Gardens* book projects. He writes a syndicated column called Family Features that's published in 160 newspapers across the country. He also writes articles as a freelance garden writer for national magazines. He regularly does television, print, and radio interviews for both the National Gardening Association and on his own. He was the host of a show on *PBS* called *Garden Smart*. He's been the gardening expert on programs such as HGTV's *Today at Home* and *Way to Grow*, the Discovery Channel's *Home Matters*, DIY's *Ask DIY*, a local Vermont show *In the Garden* as well as on QVC and The Home Shopping Network.

One of Charlie's most interesting jobs is being the Chief Gardening Officer (CGO) for the Hilton Garden Inn hotel chain. Charlie works on coordinating a program called "Grow a School Garden." Hilton Garden Inn wants to encourage children at a young age to get outside and be active, and gardening as an excellent avenue to do that. Charlie oversees partnerships between Hilton Garden Inns and local schools. The goal is to have each of the 250 Hilton Garden Inns across the country initiate a gardening project at a local school.

As a member of the Community Gardens Board for the City of Burlington, Vermont, Charlie helped ensure that the community gardens continued in perpetuity. When the program struggled with funding, Charlie recognized its importance and fought to keep it intact. Charlie says that the gardens are just "inspiring." "There is a lot of diversity of types of gardeners, but not everyone has access to land. Some people live in apartments and condos, and this is a way for them to get out, grow some of their favorite plants, and have this connection with nature and people in their community."

Throughout his career, Charlie has witnessed firsthand how gardening can bring people together, just as the community gardens in Burlington do. While working at *National Gardening Magazine*, Charlie traveled across the country in search of winners for the publication's gardening contests. "No matter what kind of political background, religion, or differences in lifestyle, when we talked about the garden, we were always on the same page. You can always meet in the garden and make a connection there." To find out more about Charlie Nardozzi and the National Gardening Association, visit their website at www.garden.org.

# Copyright Credits

*(continued from page ii)*

# More inspiration and information

The ULTIMATE DOG lover

The Best Experts' Advice for a Happy, Healthy Dog with Stories and Photos of Incredible Canines

Marty Becker, D.V.M., America's Favorite Vet
Gina Spadafori, Carol Kline, and Mikkel Becker

Code #7507 • $14.95

The ULTIMATE CAT lover

The Best Experts' Advice for a Happy, Healthy Cat with Stories and Photos of Fabulous Felines

Marty Becker, D.V.M., America's Favorite Vet
Gina Spadafori, Carol Kline, and Mikkel Becker

Code #7515 • $14.95

The ULTIMATE HORSE lover

The Best Experts' Advice for a Happy, Healthy Horse with Stories and Photos of Awe-Inspiring Equines

Marty Becker, D.V.M., America's Favorite Vet
Audrey Pavia, Gina Spadafori, and Mikkel Becker

Code #7523 • $14.95

To order direct: Telephone (800) 441-5569 • www.hcibooks.com
Prices do not include shipping and handling. Your response code is BKS.

# Collect them all